the
Longman

Reader's

Journal

the Longman *Reader's* Journal

A Guide to Reading and Thinking
to accompany the
McWhorter Reading and Study Skills Series

Academic Reading
A Brief Guide to Essential Reading Skills
College Reading and Study Skills
Efficient and Flexible Reading
Guide to College Reading
Study and Critical Thinking Skills in College
Vocabulary Simplified

the Longman *Reader's* Journal

Kathleen T. McWhorter

Niagara County Community College

Longman

New York   Boston   San Francisco
London   Toronto   Sydney   Tokyo   Singapore   Madrid
Mexico City   Munich   Paris   Cape Town   Hong Kong   Montreal

Senior Editor: Steven Rigolosi
Supplements Editor: Donna Campion
Text design and page layout: Kerry Reardon
Cover design: Maria Ilardi

THE LONGMAN READER'S JOURNAL by Kathleen T. McWhorter

ISBN: 0-321-08843-3

13 14 15 CRS 08 07

CONTENTS

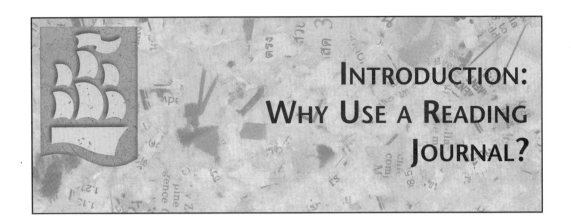

INTRODUCTION: WHY USE A READING JOURNAL?

- When given a reading assignment, are you tempted to open to the correct page and just begin reading?
- When you are finished reading, it is so easy to just close the book, isn't it?

If you want to understand and remember what you read, **this method does not work.** Instead, you must get involved before, during, and after reading. You need to think and plan before you read, read actively, and think critically and evaluate after you read.

HOW WILL THIS JOURNAL HELP ME?

This journal is intended to help you work through the reading selections in your main text. Each journal entry will guide you in getting ready to read, reading, and thinking and evaluating after you read. Yes, working though a journal entry will take longer than just reading. It might even take twice as long! However, the benefits will be well worth your time. You will find that you understand much more of what you read and that you can remember the main points of the selection after reading it. The journal entries force you to stay with the reading and maintain your concentration. They offer a systematic approach to reading. You will feel prepared to discuss the reading and answer questions about it. Best of all, you will discover that the journal process is simple and easy to use.

HOW IS THE JOURNAL ORGANIZED?

In this journal you will find three types of entries. One set of entries is to be used with textbook excerpts. Another set is for articles and essays, and a third set is for use with literature. You can use these for any reading assignment, either in your reading or study skills class or in any other course you are taking. (Feel free to duplicate extra journal pages if you need them.) You will also find a few blank Pages for Reflection. You can use these any way you would like or that your instructor suggests. At the end of this journal you will find a Vocabulary Log in which you can record new words from the readings and from your other courses that you intend to learn.

Be sure to refer to the following lists as you work through your journal entries:

- "Ten Ways to Read More Efficiently" (inside front cover)
- "Ten Useful Learning Strategies" (inside front cover)
- "Ten Ways to Stimulate Your Critical Thinking and Journal Writing" (inside back cover)

HOW DO I GET STARTED?

On the pages that follow you will find a Sample Student Journal Entry based on a textbook excerpt. It is an example that is intended to help you get started. Begin by reading the textbook excerpt "Mass Tourism Versus Ecotourism." Next, study the annotated and highlighted version of the same reading. Finally, study the Sample Student Journal Entry. Read through it to discover the kinds of responses that you might make in your journal.

Mass Tourism versus Ecotourism

1   The tourism industry has exploded in recent decades and the number of travelers grows year after year. Quicker, cheaper, and safer transportation to almost every corner of the globe is one reason for this growth. A second reason is the explosion in the number of the world's citizens who now have the leisure time and money to travel. The longer lives and better health of many of the world's peoples is a third reason. Finally, the global communications available everywhere make people more aware of the wondrous sites of the world and the endless activity options available to them.

2   This boom in tourism has given rise to millions of new jobs and increased economic prosperity in countries across the world. But, tourism can usher in problems along with economic benefits. The millions of additional tourists have strained the resources of many destinations, sometimes straining natural resources to the point where the initial appeal of an area is diminished and visitation to it declines. Figure 11.2 provides one tourism expert's idea of the stages that a destination may go through from beginning to decline.

When Is Tourism Too Much of a Good Thing?

3   The costs of tourism, especially its environmental and cultural costs, have led many destination residents and tourists alike to become disillusioned with mass tourism. Mass tourism to these critics of tourism's growth includes:

- the architectural pollution of tourist strips,
- the herding of tourists as if they were cattle,
- the disruption of traditional cultural events and occupations,
- the diminished natural environment and beauty of the area, and
- the low priority paid to local needs with funds used instead to increase tourism amenities to keep the community competitive in the marketplace.

4   Many of the gains of tourism are often short-term in nature. The costs, however, especially to the beauty and natural resources of an area, are more likely to be long-lived or even permanent. Too many times, nonlocal developers are the biggest winners and, when the area has become saturated and starts to decline, these developers move on

to the next trendy destination with no backward glance at the damage that may have been done.

5   So far in this chapter, we have included quite a list of problems, both environmental and cultural, that can result from tourism. What can be done to try to minimize these problems? Many efforts can be taken that help safeguard the environment and the native people of a tourism destination. These efforts are encompassed in a type of tourism that has come to be called **ecotourism**.

Ecotourism

6   Ecotourism, sometimes called "green tourism" or "alternative tourism," has evolved in reaction to the problems of mass tourism. Ecotourism is a form or philosophy of tourism that emphasizes the need to develop tourism in a manner that minimizes environmental impact and ensures that host communities gain the greatest economic and cultural benefits possible. The goal is to "integrate tourism development into a broader range of values and social concerns. (p. 11)[19]

7   Mass tourism, as opposed to ecotourism, tends to strain the environment through the development of more and more superstructure and the increasing wear and tear from the presence and actions of more and more tourists.[20] It is probably obvious to you that building lots of hotels, restaurants, roads, and airports can cause serious problems for an area's environment. For example, the construction of ski resorts in the Alps has led to mudslides and landslides that are damaging the mountainsides. How do individual tourists threaten the environment? One way is simply by blazing trails while walking through nature. One person walking through a wilderness area may not have any significant impact on the area, but 10,000 people within a short period certainly will. The simple action of trampling grass multiplied by 10,000 can lead to erosion of land. For example, several of New York State's Adirondack Mountain peaks are now bare due to hiker traffic. And driving through a natural area causes more damage. The manufacture and promotion of "off-road" vehicles may be the biggest threat to nature. To view even more remote areas, travelers and tour operators are venturing further into our national forests and parks, scaling fragile rock formations and converting dirt paths into rutted mud holds.

FIGURE 11.2
Stages of Tourism
Development.
Source: Butler, R. W. (1980).
Implications for management
of resources. *Canadian
Geographer,* 24, 5–12.

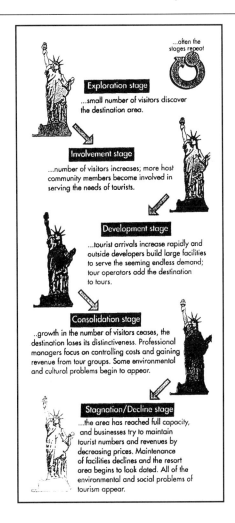

...often the
stages repeat

Exploration stage
...small number of visitors discover
the destination area.

Involvement stage
...number of visitors increases; more host
community members become involved in
serving the needs of tourists.

Development stage
...tourist arrivals increase rapidly and
outside developers build large facilities
to serve the seeming endless demand;
tour operators add the destination
to tours.

Consolidation stage
..growth in the number of visitors ceases, the
destination loses its distinctiveness. Professional
managers focus on controlling costs and gaining
revenue from tour groups. Some environmental
and cultural problems begin to appear.

Stagnation/Decline stage
...the area has reached full capacity,
and businesses try to maintain
tourist numbers and revenues by
decreasing prices. Maintenance
of facilities declines and the resort
area begins to look dated. All of the
environmental and social problems of
tourism appear.

8   As opposed to mass tourism, ecotourism primarily involves travel to sensitive natural and cultural environments to observe and learn
about a very different culture and environment and participate in low-
impact (on nature) sports such as canoeing and hiking. In addition,
ecotravelers generally desire to mingle with the local culture and have
their travel needs filled by locals in their traditional ways (such as dining on the local gastronomical delights).

9   Compared to psychocentric travelers, ecotourists tend to be wealthier, college educated, and willing to spend large amounts of money on extended trips.[21] They also tend to participate in active yet nature-focused sports such as climbing, canoeing, and kayaking.[22]

Sustaining Tourism's Benefits

10   There are five basic principles to ecotourism development.[5] The central guiding principle is that tourism should be blended with, or assimilated with, the environment and the local culture of an area. The boundary between the tourism industry and the host community should not be startling: Tourism should fit into the community and share in its ways. This blurring can occur, for example, by matching architecture to the existing local structures and using the area's natural vegetation for grounds landscaping.

11   A second principle of ecotourism is that the tourist experience should focus on the host community's exciting scenic and activity opportunities. In other words, tourism should evolve from the area's natural and historical/cultural attractions. Third, ecotourism is associated with local ownership and management of all or most services. Tourist needs should be filled by local business people and local employees rather than foreign investors or managers. In this way, more of the economic benefits of tourism flow to the local citizens and their local governments.

12   To further benefit the host community economically, the fourth principle is that a high proportion of local materials should be used to fulfill tourists' needs from construction materials to foodstuffs. For example, in Zambia, there is a unique resort called Tongabezi. the architecture of the "hotel" is a sight to behold. Most of it is built from native lumber and grasses, and many of the guestrooms are open air. One suite, called the Bird House, is built high in a huge tree and neither the bedroom nor its private bath need to have walls for modesty's sake. The height of the rooms alone provide all the privacy needed.

13   Finally, the fifth principle highlights the importance of conservation of resources. By using what are called "ecotechniques," local utilities such as water, heat, and electricity can be stretched to accommodate the needs of both the tourists and the local population. Ecotechniques include use of solar power, rain water collection, and bioclimatic design of structures to aid in heating and cooling.

14   From these five principles, host communities can gain many potential benefits that they may not gain from mass tourism, including:

- generating more income for more local community members,
- promoting understanding between locals and members of different cultures,
- educating local populations of matters of health, education, energy use, business, and environmental conservation, and
- providing a financial incentive to protect and conserve a globally significant natural/cultural resource.

15   Ecotourism and ecotechniques can be used by newly developed and fully developed tourist destinations to try to minimize the negative impacts that large numbers of visitors can have on host communities and the environment. At the dawn of the 21st century, more and more nations and communities will need to apply the principles of ecotourism and conservation to ensure that the tourism industry of the area remains viable.

16   Ecotourism will not replace the ever-growing demand for mass tourism, but it can teach us some valuable lessons. Unchecked and unplanned tourism growth can lead to the eventual destruction of the very assets that originally served to attract visitors. Taking steps to preserve and protect tourist attractions will create a legacy for future generations.

Mass Tourism versus Ecotourism

1   The underline{tourism industry has exploded} in recent decades and the number of travelers grows year after year. ①underline{Quicker, cheaper, and safer transportation} to almost every corner of the globe is one reason for this growth. A second reason is the explosion in the ②underline{number of the world's citizens} who now have the leisure time and money to travel. The ③underline{longer lives and better health} of many of the world's peoples is a third reason. Finally, the ④underline{global communications} available everywhere make people more aware of the wondrous sites of the world and the endless activity options available to them.

2   This boom in tourism has given rise to millions of underline{new jobs} and underline{increased economic prosperity} in countries across the world. But, tourism can usher in problems along with economic benefits. The millions of additional tourists have strained the resources of many destinations, sometimes underline{straining natural resources} to the point where the initial appeal of an area is diminished and underline{visitation to it declines}. Figure 11.2 provides one tourism expert's idea of the stages that a destination may go through from beginning to decline.

When Is Tourism Too Much of a Good Thing?

3   The costs of tourism, especially its environmental and cultural costs, have led many destination residents and tourists alike to become disillusioned with mass tourism. Mass tourism to these critics of tourism's growth includes:

- the architectural pollution of tourist strips,
- the herding of tourists as if they were cattle,
- the disruption of traditional cultural events and occupations,
- the diminished natural environment and beauty of the area, and
- the low priority paid to local needs with funds used instead to increase tourism amenities to keep the community competitive in the marketplace.

4   Many of the underline{gains} of tourism are often underline{short-term} in nature. The underline{costs,} however, especially to the beauty and natural resources of an area, are more likely to be underline{long-lived or even permanent.} Too many times, nonlocal developers are the biggest winners and, when the area has become saturated and starts to decline, these developers move on

Margin annotations:

4 reasons for expansion of tourism

benefit

problem

effects of mass tourism

to the next trendy destination with no backward glance at the damage that may have been done.

So far in this chapter, we have included quite a list of problems, both environmental and cultural, that can result from tourism. What can be done to try to minimize these problems? Many efforts can be taken that help safeguard the environment and the native people of a tourism destination. These efforts are encompassed in a type of tourism that has come to be called **ecotourism**.

Ecotourism

definition

Ecotourism, sometimes called "green tourism" or "alternative tourism," has evolved in reaction to the problems of mass tourism. Ecotourism is a form or philosophy of tourism that emphasizes the need to develop tourism in a manner that minimizes environmental impact and ensures that host communities gain the greatest economic and cultural benefits possible. The goal is to "integrate tourism development into a broader range of values and social concerns. (p. 11)

Mass tourism, as opposed to ecotourism, tends to strain the environment through the development of more and more superstructure and the increasing wear and tear from the presence and actions of more and more tourists.[20] It is probably obvious to you that building lots of hotels, restaurants, roads, and airports can cause serious problems for an area's environment. For example, the construction of

example of effect of mass tourism

ski resorts in the Alps has led to mudslides and landslides that are damaging the mountainsides. How do individual tourists threaten the environment? One way is simply by blazing trails while walking through nature. One person walking through a wilderness area may not have any significant impact on the area, but 10,000 people within in a short period certainly will. The simple action of trampling grass multiplied by 10,000 can lead to erosion of land. For example, several of New York State's Adirondack Mountain peaks are now bare due to hiker traffic. And driving through a natural area causes more dam-

example of destruction

age. The manufacture and promotion of "off-road" vehicles may be the biggest threat to nature. To view even more remote areas, travelers and tour operators are venturing further into our national forests and parks, scaling fragile rock formations and converting dirt paths into rutted mud holds.

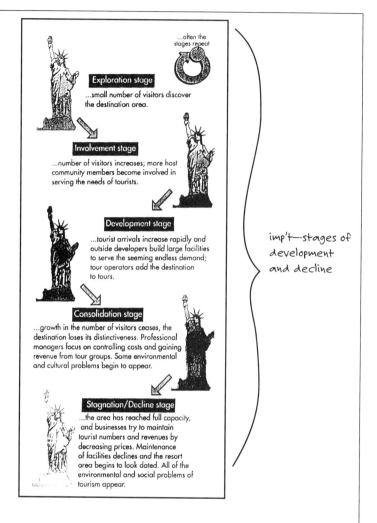

FIGURE 11.2
Stages of Tourism Development.
Source: Butler, R. W. (1980). Implications for management of resources. *Canadian Geographer*, 24, 5–12.

Exploration stage
...small number of visitors discover the destination area.

...often the stages repeat

Involvement stage
...number of visitors increases; more host community members become involved in serving the needs of tourists.

Development stage
...tourist arrivals increase rapidly and outside developers build large facilities to serve the seeming endless demand; tour operators add the destination to tours.

Consolidation stage
...growth in the number of visitors ceases, the destination loses its distinctiveness. Professional managers focus on controlling costs and gaining revenue from tour groups. Some environmental and cultural problems begin to appear.

Stagnation/Decline stage
...the area has reached full capacity, and businesses try to maintain tourist numbers and revenues by decreasing prices. Maintenance of facilities declines and the resort area begins to look dated. All of the environmental and social problems of tourism appear.

imp't—stages of development and decline

8   As opposed to mass tourism, <u>ecotourism primarily involves</u> travel to sensitive natural and cultural environments to observe and <u>learn about a very different culture</u> and environment and <u>participate in low-impact (on nature) sports</u> such as canoeing and hiking. In addition, **ecotravelers** generally desire to <u>mingle with the local culture</u> and have their <u>travel needs filled by locals</u> in their traditional ways (such as dining on the local gastronomical delights).

9   Compared to psychocentric travelers, **ecotourists** tend to be wealthier, college educated, and willing to spend large amounts of money on extended trips.[21] They also tend to participate in active yet nature-focused sports such as climbing, canoeing, and kayaking.[22]

Sustaining Tourism's Benefits

5 principles of 10   There are <u>five basic principles</u> to <u>ecotourism development.</u>[5] The cen-
ecotourism   tral guiding principle is that tourism should be <u>blended with,</u> or assim-
                 ilated with, <u>the environment</u> and the local culture of an area. The ①
                 boundary between the tourism industry and the host community should not be startling: Tourism should fit into the community and share in its ways. This blurring can occur, for example, by matching architecture to the existing local structures and using the area's natural vegetation for grounds landscaping.

11   A second principle of ecotourism is that the tourist experience ②
                 should <u>focus on</u> the <u>host community's exciting scenic and activity oppor-
                 tunities.</u> In other words, tourism should evolve from the area's natural and historical/cultural attractions. Third, ecotourism is associated with <u>local ownership and management of all or most services.</u> Tourist needs ③ should be filled by local business people and local employees rather than foreign investors or managers. In this way, more of the economic bene-fits of tourism flow to the local citizens and their local governments.

12   To further benefit the host community economically, the fourth principle is that a <u>high proportion of local materials should be used to</u> ④
                 <u>fulfill tourists'</u> needs from construction materials to foodstuffs. For
ex.   example, in Zambia, there is a unique resort called Tongabezi. the architecture of the "hotel" is a sight to behold. Most of it is built from native lumber and grasses, and many of the guestrooms are open air. One suite, called the Bird House, is built high in a huge tree and nei-ther the bedroom nor its private bath need to have walls for modesty's sake. the height of the rooms alone provide all the privacy needed.

13   Finally, the fifth principle highlights the importance of <u>conser-</u>
def.   <u>vation of resources.</u> By using what are called "ecotechniques," <u>local</u> ⑤
                 <u>utilities</u> such as water, heat, and electricity can be stretched to accom-modate the needs of both the tourists and the local population. Ecotechniques include use of <u>solar power</u>, <u>rain water collection</u>, and <u>bioclimatic design of structures</u> to aid in heating and cooling.

14   From these five principles, host communities can gain many potential benefits that they may not gain from mass tourism, including:

benefits of ecotourism

- generating more income for more local community members,
- promoting understanding between locals and members of different cultures,
- educating local populations on matters of health, education, energy use, business, and environmental conservation, and
- providing a financial incentive to protect and conserve a globally significant natural/cultural resource.

15   Ecotourism and ecotechniques can be used by newly developed and fully developed tourist destinations to try to minimize the negative impacts that large numbers of visitors can have on host communities and the environment. At the dawn of the 21st century, more and more nations and communities will need to apply the principles of ecotourism and conservation to ensure that the tourism industry of the area remains viable.

16   Ecotourism will not replace the ever-growing demand for mass tourism, but it can teach us some valuable lessons. Unchecked and unplanned tourism growth can lead to the eventual destruction of the very assets that originally served to attract visitors. Taking steps to preserve and protect tourist attractions will create a legacy for future generations.

JOURNAL ENTRY FOR A TEXTBOOK

Textbook Reading: <u>Mass Tourism Versus Ecotourism</u> _____ <u>5/26/00</u>
(title)   (page)   (date)

Academic Discipline: <u>Careers</u> _____

BEFORE READING

1. **PREREADING.** After you have preread the selection, describe the topics and ideas you expect it to cover. Choose one of the following methods:
   - write list of topics you expect the reading to cover
   - write a list of questions you expect the reading to answer
   - draw a diagram or map identifying key topics
   - discuss your prereading with a classmate; summarize the ideas you predict the reading will explore.

   <u>What is ecotourism?</u>

   <u>What problems have mass tourism created?</u>

   <u>What are the stages tourism development follows?</u>

   <u>What are tourism's benefits?</u>

2. **CHOOSING A TEXTBOOK READING STRATEGY.** Based on what you discovered from your prereading, decide how you will read the selection. What strategies will you use? (See the inside front cover for a list of learning strategies.) Record your choice(s) below.

   Learning Strategies: 1. <u>highlight</u>

   2. <u>summarize</u>

   3. <u>reread difficult sections</u>

WHILE READING

3. **MARKING UNFAMILIAR VOCABULARY.** Use context, word parts, or a dictionary to find the meanings. Jot the words' meanings as brief notes in the margin.

AFTER READING:

4. **LEARNING VOCABULARY.** Using either index cards or the Vocabulary Log beginning on p. 00, record the unfamiliar words you marked along with their meanings.

5. **EVALUATING YOUR TEXTBOOK READING STRATEGIES.** Did the learning strategies you chose in #2 above work? Write a few sentences describing what did or did not work. If a strategy did not work, try to think of reasons. What, if anything, was troublesome in the reading? Explore possible solutions.

    Highlighting worked well because topic sentences and details

    were easy to find. Summarizing forced me to take another

    look at the whold reading.

    The reading was not as difficult as I anticipated, so I did not

    need to reread.

6.   **THINKING CRITICALLY.**   Use the following two-column journal to spur your thinking about the reading. In the left column record statements or paraphrased ideas from the reading that you want to explore. In the right column, write your reactions, comments, or questions. Feel free to disagree, challenge, and offer alternative viewpoints. See the inside back cover of this journal for "Ten Ways to Stimulate Your Critical Thinking and Journal Writing."

READING SELECTION	YOUR RESPONSE
global communications have made people more aware of tourist sites (Para. 1)	What type of communication—the Internet? Isn't it possible that greater opportunities to view and learn about tourist sites might decrease the need to visit them?
Stages of tourism— (Para. 2)	—reminds me of Niagara Falls—an example would help here—Explain what happened to a particular place at each stage.
"herding of tourists as if they were cattle" (Para. 3)	Why do people put up with this? Doesn't this discourage tourism?
"How do individual tourists threaten the environment?" (Para. 7)	The author answers this but does not discuss how tourists can damage the native people by prying into their lives and disrupting their lives.
Tourist businesses should be locally owned (Para. 11)	How can local people afford to build hotels, etc. Should governments offer help?
example of resort in Zambia (Para. 12)	—would be fabulous place to visit! —more of these examples would help me understand what ecotourism really is
"communities will need to apply principles of ecotourism." (Para. 15)	What incentives would help them do so?

7. **CHOOSING A LEARNING STRATEGY.** Assume you had to take an exam based on this textbook excerpt. What learning strategies would you use?

    Learning Strategies: 1. _review highlighting_

    2. _prepare a study sheet_

    3. _____

8. **PREDICTING AN ESSAY EXAM QUESTION.** Assume you were going to take an essay exam based, in part, on this excerpt. What question(s) would you predict?

    Essay Exam Questions: 1. _Define ecotourism and explain the_

    2. _principles on which its development_

    3. _is based_

9. **RATING THE READING.** Alone or working with a classmate, evaluate and rate the reading selection according to each of the following criteria. Use a scale of 1 to 5, with 1 being the lowest rating and 5 being the highest rating. (1=strongly disagree, 2=disagree, 3=uncertain, 4=agree, 5=strongly agree)

CRITERIA	YOUR RATING
a. The reading was interesting and informative.	4
b. The author made it clear what was important.	5
c. The author provided helpful examples and explanations.	2
d. The reading was well organized.	4
e. The author defined specialized or technical vocabulary.	3

10. **FURTHER DISCUSSION, READING, AND RESEARCH.** What questions would you like to ask the author? What topics or ideas do you want to know more about?

    I would like to read more about places to visit that are still

    unspoiled by tourists.

    How do the natives of Zambia feel about the Tongavezi resort?

JOURNAL ENTRIES
FOR TEXTBOOKS

JOURNAL ENTRY FOR A TEXTBOOK–1

Textbook Reading: _____ _____ _____
(title)   (page)   (date)

Academic Discipline: _____

BEFORE READING

1.   **PREREADING.** After you have preread the selection, describe the topics
     and ideas you expect it to cover. Choose one of the following methods:
     • write a list of topics you expect the reading to cover
     • write a list of questions you expect the reading to answer
     • draw a diagram or map identifying key topics
     • discuss your prereading with a classmate; summarize the ideas you
       predict the reading will explore.

     _____

     _____

     _____

     _____

2.   **CHOOSING A TEXTBOOK READING STRATEGY.** Based on what you
     discovered from your prereading, decide how you will read the selection.
     What strategies will you use? (See the inside front cover for a list of
     learning strategies.) Record your choice(s) below.

     Learning Strategies: 1. _____

                               2. _____

                               3. _____

WHILE READING

3.   **MARKING UNFAMILIAR VOCABULARY.** Use context, word parts, or a dictionary to find the meanings. Jot the words' meanings as brief notes in the margin.

AFTER READING:

4.   **LEARNING VOCABULARY.** Using either index cards or the Vocabulary Log beginning on p. 165, record the unfamiliar words you marked along with their meanings.

5.   **EVALUATING YOUR TEXTBOOK READING STRATEGIES.** Did the learning strategies you chose in #2 work? Write a few sentences describing what did or did not work. If a strategy did not work, try to think of reasons. What, if anything, was troublesome in the reading? Explore possible solutions.

_____

_____

_____

_____

_____

_____

_____

_____

_____

_____

_____

6. **THINKING CRITICALLY.**   Use the following two-column journal to spur your thinking about the reading. In the left column record statements or paraphrased ideas from the reading that you want to explore. In the right column, write your reactions, comments, or questions. Feel free to disagree, challenge, and offer alternative viewpoints. See the inside back cover of this journal for "Ten Ways to Stimulate Your Critical Thinking and Journal Writing."

Textbooks

READING SELECTION	YOUR RESPONSE
(Para. __)	
(Para. __)	
(Para. __)	
(Para. __)	
(Para. __)	
(Para. __)	
(Para. __)	

7.   **CHOOSING A LEARNING STRATEGY.** Assume you had to take an exam based on this textbook excerpt. What learning strategies would you use?

     Learning Strategies: 1. _____

                                  2. _____

                                    3. _____

8.   **PREDICTING AN ESSAY EXAM QUESTION.** Assume you were going to take an essay exam based, in part, on this excerpt. What question(s) would you predict?

     Essay Exam Questions: 1. _____

                                    2. _____

                                    3. _____

9.   **RATING THE READING.** Alone or working with a classmate, evaluate and rate the reading selection according to each of the following criteria. Use a scale of 1 to 5, with 1 being the lowest rating and 5 being the highest rating. (1=strongly disagree, 2=disagree, 3=uncertain, 4=agree, 5=strongly agree)

CRITERIA	YOUR RATING
a. The reading was interesting and informative.	_____
b. The author made it clear what was important.	_____
c. The author provided helpful examples and explanations.	_____
d. The reading was well organized.	_____
e. The author defined specialized or technical vocabulary	_____

10.   **FURTHER DISCUSSION, READING, AND RESEARCH.** What questions would you like to ask the author? What topics or ideas do you want to know more about?

_____

_____

_____

_____

_____

JOURNAL ENTRY FOR A TEXTBOOK–2

Textbook Reading: _____ _____ _____
(title)   (page)   (date)

Academic Discipline: _____

BEFORE READING

1. **PREREADING.** After you have preread the selection, describe the topics and ideas you expect it to cover. Choose one of the following methods:
   - write a list of topics you expect the reading to cover
   - write a list of questions you expect the reading to answer
   - draw a diagram or map identifying key topics
   - discuss your prereading with a classmate; summarize the ideas you predict the reading will explore.

   _____

   _____

   _____

   _____

2. **CHOOSING A TEXTBOOK READING STRATEGY.** Based on what you discovered from your prereading, decide how you will read the selection. What strategies will you use? (See the inside front cover for a list of learning strategies.) Record your choice(s) below.

   Learning Strategies: 1. _____

   2. _____

   3. _____

WHILE READING

3.   **MARKING UNFAMILIAR VOCABULARY.** Use context, word parts, or a dictionary to find the meanings. Jot the words' meanings as brief notes in the margin.

AFTER READING:

4.   **LEARNING VOCABULARY.** Using either index cards or the Vocabulary Log beginning on p. 165, record the unfamiliar words you marked along with their meanings.

5.   **EVALUATING YOUR TEXTBOOK READING STRATEGIES.**   Did the learning strategies you chose in #2 work? Write a few sentences describing what did or did not work. If a strategy did not work, try to think of reasons. What, if anything, was troublesome in the reading?   Explore possible solutions.

_____

_____

_____

_____

_____

_____

_____

_____

_____

_____

6. **THINKING CRITICALLY.** Use the following two-column journal to spur your thinking about the reading. In the left column record statements or paraphrased ideas from the reading that you want to explore. In the right column, write your reactions, comments, or questions. Feel free to disagree, challenge, and offer alternative viewpoints. See the inside back cover of this journal for "Ten Ways to Stimulate Your Critical Thinking and Journal Writing."

Textbooks

READING SELECTION	YOUR RESPONSE
(Para. __)	
(Para. __)	
(Para. __)	
(Para. __)	
(Para. __)	
(Para. __)	
(Para. __)	

7.   **CHOOSING A LEARNING STRATEGY.** Assume you had to take an exam based on this textbook excerpt. What learning strategies would you use?

Learning Strategies: 1. _____

2. _____

3. _____

8.   **PREDICTING AN ESSAY EXAM QUESTION.** Assume you were going to take an essay exam based, in part, on this excerpt. What question(s) would you predict?

Essay Exam Questions: 1. _____

2. _____

3. _____

9.   **RATING THE READING.** Alone or working with a classmate, evaluate and rate the reading selection according to each of the following criteria. Use a scale of 1 to 5, with 1 being the lowest rating and 5 being the highest rating. (1=strongly disagree, 2=disagree, 3=uncertain, 4=agree, 5=strongly agree)

CRITERIA	YOUR RATING
a. The reading was interesting and informative.	_____
b. The author made it clear what was important.	_____
c. The author provided helpful examples and explanations.	_____
d. The reading was well organized.	_____
e. The author defined specialized or technical vocabulary	_____

10.   **FURTHER DISCUSSION, READING, AND RESEARCH.** What questions would you like to ask the author? What topics or ideas do you want to know more about?

_____

_____

_____

_____

_____

JOURNAL ENTRY FOR A TEXTBOOK–3

Textbook Reading: _____ _____ _____
(title)   (page)   (date)

Academic Discipline: _____

BEFORE READING

1. **PREREADING.** After you have preread the selection, describe the topics and ideas you expect it to cover. Choose one of the following methods:
   - write a list of topics you expect the reading to cover
   - write a list of questions you expect the reading to answer
   - draw a diagram or map identifying key topics
   - discuss your prereading with a classmate; summarize the ideas you predict the reading will explore.

   _____

   _____

   _____

   _____

2. **CHOOSING A TEXTBOOK READING STRATEGY.** Based on what you discovered from your prereading, decide how you will read the selection. What strategies will you use? (See the inside front cover for a list of learning strategies.) Record your choice(s) below.

   Learning Strategies: 1. _____

   2. _____

   3. _____

WHILE READING

3. **MARKING UNFAMILIAR VOCABULARY.** Use context, word parts, or a dictionary to find the meanings. Jot the words' meanings as brief notes in the margin.

AFTER READING:

4. **LEARNING VOCABULARY.** Using either index cards or the Vocabulary Log beginning on p. 165, record the unfamiliar words you marked along with their meanings.

5. **EVALUATING YOUR TEXTBOOK READING STRATEGIES.** Did the learning strategies you chose in #2 work? Write a few sentences describing what did or did not work. If a strategy did not work, try to think of reasons. What, if anything, was troublesome in the reading? Explore possible solutions.

_____

_____

_____

_____

_____

_____

_____

_____

_____

_____

_____

_____

6.   **THINKING CRITICALLY.**   Use the following two-column journal to spur your thinking about the reading. In the left column record statements or paraphrased ideas from the reading that you want to explore. In the right column, write your reactions, comments, or questions. Feel free to disagree, challenge, and offer alternative viewpoints. See the inside back cover of this journal for "Ten Ways to Stimulate Your Critical Thinking and Journal Writing."

READING SELECTION	YOUR RESPONSE
(Para. __)	
(Para. __)	
(Para. __)	
(Para. __)	
(Para. __)	
(Para. __)	
(Para. __)	

7. **CHOOSING A LEARNING STRATEGY.** Assume you had to take an exam based on this textbook excerpt. What learning strategies would you use?

   Learning Strategies: 1. _____

   2. _____

   3. _____

8. **PREDICTING AN ESSAY EXAM QUESTION.** Assume you were going to take an essay exam based, in part, on this excerpt. What question(s) would you predict?

   Essay Exam Questions: 1. _____

   2. _____

   3. _____

9. **RATING THE READING.** Alone or working with a classmate, evaluate and rate the reading selection according to each of the following criteria. Use a scale of 1 to 5, with 1 being the lowest rating and 5 being the highest rating. (1=strongly disagree, 2=disagree, 3=uncertain, 4=agree, 5=strongly agree)

CRITERIA	YOUR RATING
a. The reading was interesting and informative.	_____
b. The author made it clear what was important.	_____
c. The author provided helpful examples and explanations.	_____
d. The reading was well organized.	_____
e. The author defined specialized or technical vocabulary	_____

10. **FURTHER DISCUSSION, READING, AND RESEARCH.** What questions would you like to ask the author? What topics or ideas do you want to know more about?

    _____

    _____

    _____

    _____

    _____

JOURNAL ENTRY FOR A TEXTBOOK–4

Textbook Reading: _____ _____ _____
(title) (page) (date)

Academic Discipline: _____

BEFORE READING

1. **PREREADING.** After you have preread the selection, describe the topics and ideas you expect it to cover. Choose one of the following methods:
    - write a list of topics you expect the reading to cover
    - write a list of questions you expect the reading to answer
    - draw a diagram or map identifying key topics
    - discuss your prereading with a classmate; summarize the ideas you predict the reading will explore.

    _____

    _____

    _____

    _____

2. **CHOOSING A TEXTBOOK READING STRATEGY.** Based on what you discovered from your prereading, decide how you will read the selection. What strategies will you use? (See the inside front cover for a list of learning strategies.) Record your choice(s) below.

    Learning Strategies: 1. _____

    2. _____

    3. _____

WHILE READING

3.   **MARKING UNFAMILIAR VOCABULARY.** Use context, word parts, or a dictionary to find the meanings. Jot the words' meanings as brief notes in the margin.

AFTER READING:

4.   **LEARNING VOCABULARY.** Using either index cards or the Vocabulary Log beginning on p. 165, record the unfamiliar words you marked along with their meanings.

5.   **EVALUATING YOUR TEXTBOOK READING STRATEGIES.** Did the learning strategies you chose in #2 work? Write a few sentences describing what did or did not work. If a strategy did not work, try to think of reasons. What, if anything, was troublesome in the reading? Explore possible solutions.

_____

_____

_____

_____

_____

_____

_____

_____

_____

_____

_____

_____

6. **THINKING CRITICALLY.** Use the following two-column journal to spur your thinking about the reading. In the left column record statements or paraphrased ideas from the reading that you want to explore. In the right column, write your reactions, comments, or questions. Feel free to disagree, challenge, and offer alternative viewpoints. See the inside back cover of this journal for "Ten Ways to Stimulate Your Critical Thinking and Journal Writing."

READING SELECTION	YOUR RESPONSE
(Para. ___)	
(Para. ___)	
(Para. ___)	
(Para. ___)	
(Para. ___)	
(Para. ___)	
(Para. ___)	

Textbooks

7.   **CHOOSING A LEARNING STRATEGY.** Assume you had to take an exam based on this textbook excerpt. What learning strategies would you use?

Learning Strategies: 1. _____

2. _____

3. _____

8.   **PREDICTING AN ESSAY EXAM QUESTION.** Assume you were going to take an essay exam based, in part, on this excerpt. What question(s) would you predict?

Essay Exam Questions: 1. _____

2. _____

3. _____

9.   **RATING THE READING.** Alone or working with a classmate, evaluate and rate the reading selection according to each of the following criteria. Use a scale of 1 to 5, with 1 being the lowest rating and 5 being the highest rating. (1=strongly disagree, 2=disagree, 3=uncertain, 4=agree, 5=strongly agree)

	CRITERIA	YOUR RATING
a.	The reading was interesting and informative.	_____
b.	The author made it clear what was important.	_____
c.	The author provided helpful examples and explanations.	_____
d.	The reading was well organized.	_____
e.	The author defined specialized or technical vocabulary	_____

10.   **FURTHER DISCUSSION, READING, AND RESEARCH.** What questions would you like to ask the author? What topics or ideas do you want to know more about?

_____

_____

_____

_____

_____

JOURNAL ENTRY FOR A TEXTBOOK–5

Textbook Reading: _____ _____ _____
                                        (title)   (page)   (date)

Academic Discipline: _____

BEFORE READING

1. **PREREADING.** After you have preread the selection, describe the topics
    and ideas you expect it to cover. Choose one of the following methods:
    • write a list of topics you expect the reading to cover
    • write a list of questions you expect the reading to answer
    • draw a diagram or map identifying key topics
    • discuss your prereading with a classmate; summarize the ideas you
      predict the reading will explore.

    _____

    _____

    _____

    _____

2. **CHOOSING A TEXTBOOK READING STRATEGY.** Based on what you
    discovered from your prereading, decide how you will read the selection.
    What strategies will you use? (See the inside front cover for a list of
    learning strategies.) Record your choice(s) below.

    Learning Strategies: 1. _____

                               2. _____

                               3. _____

WHILE READING

3. **MARKING UNFAMILIAR VOCABULARY.** Use context, word parts, or a dictionary to find the meanings. Jot the words' meanings as brief notes in the margin.

AFTER READING:

4. **LEARNING VOCABULARY.** Using either index cards or the Vocabulary Log beginning on p. 165, record the unfamiliar words you marked along with their meanings.

5. **EVALUATING YOUR TEXTBOOK READING STRATEGIES.** Did the learning strategies you chose in #2 above work? Write a few sentences describing what did or did not work. If a strategy did not work, try to think of reasons. What, if anything, was troublesome in the reading? Explore possible solutions.

_____

_____

_____

_____

_____

_____

_____

_____

_____

_____

_____

6.   **THINKING CRITICALLY.**   Use the following two-column journal to spur your thinking about the reading. In the left column record statements or paraphrased ideas from the reading that you want to explore. In the right column, write your reactions, comments, or questions. Feel free to disagree, challenge, and offer alternative viewpoints. See the inside back cover of this journal for "Ten Ways to Stimulate Your Critical Thinking and Journal Writing."

READING SELECTION	YOUR RESPONSE
(Para. __)	
(Para. __)	
(Para. __)	
(Para. __)	
(Para. __)	
(Para. __)	
(Para. __)	

7.   CHOOSING A LEARNING STRATEGY. Assume you had to take an exam based on this textbook excerpt. What learning strategies would you use?

Learning Strategies: 1. _____

2. _____

3. _____

8.   PREDICTING AN ESSAY EXAM QUESTION. Assume you were going to take an essay exam based, in part, on this excerpt. What question(s) would you predict?

Essay Exam Questions: 1. _____

2. _____

3. _____

9.   RATING THE READING. Alone or working with a classmate, evaluate and rate the reading selection according to each of the following criteria. Use a scale of 1 to 5, with 1 being the lowest rating and 5 being the highest rating. (1=strongly disagree, 2=disagree, 3=uncertain, 4=agree, 5=strongly agree)

CRITERIA	YOUR RATING
a. The reading was interesting and informative.	_____
b. The author made it clear what was important.	_____
c. The author provided helpful examples and explanations.	_____
d. The reading was well organized.	_____
e. The author defined specialized or technical vocabulary	_____

10.   FURTHER DISCUSSION, READING, AND RESEARCH. What questions would you like to ask the author? What topics or ideas do you want to know more about?

_____

_____

_____

_____

_____

JOURNAL ENTRY FOR A TEXTBOOK–6

Textbook Reading: _____ _____ _____
(title)   (page)   (date)

Academic Discipline: _____

BEFORE READING

1. **PREREADING.** After you have preread the selection, describe the topics and ideas you expect it to cover. Choose one of the following methods:
   - write a list of topics you expect the reading to cover
   - write a list of questions you expect the reading to answer
   - draw a diagram or map identifying key topics
   - discuss your prereading with a classmate; summarize the ideas you predict the reading will explore.

   _____

   _____

   _____

   _____

2. **CHOOSING A TEXTBOOK READING STRATEGY.** Based on what you discovered from your prereading, decide how you will read the selection. What strategies will you use? (See the inside front cover for a list of learning strategies.) Record your choice(s) below.

   Learning Strategies: 1. _____

   2. _____

   3. _____

WHILE READING

3.   **MARKING UNFAMILIAR VOCABULARY.** Use context, word parts, or a dictionary to find the meanings. Jot the words' meanings as brief notes in the margin.

AFTER READING:

4.   **LEARNING VOCABULARY.** Using either index cards or the Vocabulary Log beginning on p. 165, record the unfamiliar words you marked along with their meanings.

5.   **EVALUATING YOUR TEXTBOOK READING STRATEGIES.** Did the learning strategies you chose in #2 work? Write a few sentences describing what did or did not work. If a strategy did not work, try to think of reasons. What, if anything, was troublesome in the reading? Explore possible solutions.

_____

_____

_____

_____

_____

_____

_____

_____

_____

_____

6.   **THINKING CRITICALLY.**   Use the following two-column journal to spur your thinking about the reading. In the left column record statements or paraphrased ideas from the reading that you want to explore. In the right column, write your reactions, comments, or questions. Feel free to disagree, challenge, and offer alternative viewpoints. See the inside back cover of this journal for "Ten Ways to Stimulate Your Critical Thinking and Journal Writing."

READING SELECTION	YOUR RESPONSE
(Para. __)	
(Para. __)	
(Para. __)	
(Para. __)	
(Para. __)	
(Para. __)	
(Para. __)	

Textbooks

7.   **CHOOSING A LEARNING STRATEGY.** Assume you had to take an exam based on this textbook excerpt. What learning strategies would you use?

Learning Strategies: 1. _____

2. _____

3. _____

8.   **PREDICTING AN ESSAY EXAM QUESTION.** Assume you were going to take an essay exam based, in part, on this excerpt. What question(s) would you predict?

Essay Exam Questions: 1. _____

2. _____

3. _____

9.   **RATING THE READING.** Alone or working with a classmate, evaluate and rate the reading selection according to each of the following criteria. Use a scale of 1 to 5, with 1 being the lowest rating and 5 being the highest rating. (1=strongly disagree, 2=disagree, 3=uncertain, 4=agree, 5=strongly agree)

CRITERIA	YOUR RATING
a. The reading was interesting and informative.	_____
b. The author made it clear what was important.	_____
c. The author provided helpful examples and explanations.	_____
d. The reading was well organized.	_____
e. The author defined specialized or technical vocabulary	_____

10.   **FURTHER DISCUSSION, READING, AND RESEARCH.** What questions would you like to ask the author? What topics or ideas do you want to know more about?

_____

_____

_____

_____

_____

JOURNAL ENTRY FOR A TEXTBOOK-7

Textbook Reading: _____ _____ _____
(title)   (page)   (date)

Academic Discipline: _____

BEFORE READING

1. **PREREADING.** After you have preread the selection, describe the topics and ideas you expect it to cover. Choose one of the following methods:
    - write a list of topics you expect the reading to cover
    - write a list of questions you expect the reading to answer
    - draw a diagram or map identifying key topics
    - discuss your prereading with a classmate; summarize the ideas you predict the reading will explore.

    _____

    _____

    _____

    _____

2. **CHOOSING A TEXTBOOK READING STRATEGY.** Based on what you discovered from your prereading, decide how you will read the selection. What strategies will you use? (See the inside front cover for a list of learning strategies.) Record your choice(s) below.

    Learning Strategies: 1. _____

    2. _____

    3. _____

WHILE READING

3. **MARKING UNFAMILIAR VOCABULARY.** Use context, word parts, or a dictionary to find the meanings. Jot the words' meanings as brief notes in the margin.

AFTER READING:

4. **LEARNING VOCABULARY.** Using either index cards or the Vocabulary Log beginning on p. 165, record the unfamiliar words you marked along with their meanings.

5. **EVALUATING YOUR TEXTBOOK READING STRATEGIES.** Did the learning strategies you chose in #2 work? Write a few sentences describing what did or did not work. If a strategy did not work, try to think of reasons. What, if anything, was troublesome in the reading? Explore possible solutions.

_____

_____

_____

_____

_____

_____

_____

_____

_____

_____

_____

6. **THINKING CRITICALLY.** Use the following two-column journal to spur your thinking about the reading. In the left column record statements or paraphrased ideas from the reading that you want to explore. In the right column, write your reactions, comments, or questions. Feel free to disagree, challenge, and offer alternative viewpoints. See the inside back cover of this journal for "Ten Ways to Stimulate Your Critical Thinking and Journal Writing."

READING SELECTION	YOUR RESPONSE
(Para. __)	
(Para. __)	
(Para. __)	
(Para. __)	
(Para. __)	
(Para. __)	
(Para. __)	

Textbooks

7. **CHOOSING A LEARNING STRATEGY.** Assume you had to take an exam based on this textbook excerpt. What learning strategies would you use?

   Learning Strategies: 1. _____

   2. _____

   3. _____

8. **PREDICTING AN ESSAY EXAM QUESTION.** Assume you were going to take an essay exam based, in part, on this excerpt. What question(s) would you predict?

   Essay Exam Questions: 1. _____

   2. _____

   3. _____

9. **RATING THE READING.** Alone or working with a classmate, evaluate and rate the reading selection according to each of the following criteria. Use a scale of 1 to 5, with 1 being the lowest rating and 5 being the highest rating. (1=strongly disagree, 2=disagree, 3=uncertain, 4=agree, 5=strongly agree)

CRITERIA	YOUR RATING
a. The reading was interesting and informative.	_____
b. The author made it clear what was important.	_____
c. The author provided helpful examples and explanations.	_____
d. The reading was well organized.	_____
e. The author defined specialized or technical vocabulary	_____

10. **FURTHER DISCUSSION, READING, AND RESEARCH.** What questions would you like to ask the author? What topics or ideas do you want to know more about?

    _____

    _____

    _____

    _____

    _____

JOURNAL ENTRY FOR A TEXTBOOK–8

Textbook Reading: _____ _____ _____
(title)   (page)   (date)

Academic Discipline: _____

BEFORE READING

1. **PREREADING.** After you have preread the selection, describe the topics
    and ideas you expect it to cover. Choose one of the following methods:
    *   write a list of topics you expect the reading to cover
    *   write a list of questions you expect the reading to answer
    *   draw a diagram or map identifying key topics
    *   discuss your prereading with a classmate; summarize the ideas you
        predict the reading will explore.

    _____

    _____

    _____

    _____

2. **CHOOSING A TEXTBOOK READING STRATEGY.** Based on what you
    discovered from your prereading, decide how you will read the selection.
    What strategies will you use? (See the inside front cover for a list of
    learning strategies.) Record your choice(s) below.

    Learning Strategies: 1. _____

    2. _____

    3. _____

WHILE READING

3.   **MARKING UNFAMILIAR VOCABULARY.** Use context, word parts, or a dictionary to find the meanings. Jot the words' meanings as brief notes in the margin.

AFTER READING:

4.   **LEARNING VOCABULARY.** Using either index cards or the Vocabulary Log beginning on p. 165, record the unfamiliar words you marked along with their meanings.

5.   **EVALUATING YOUR TEXTBOOK READING STRATEGIES.**   Did the learning strategies you chose in #2 work? Write a few sentences describing what did or did not work. If a strategy did not work, try to think of reasons. What, if anything, was troublesome in the reading?   Explore possible solutions.

_____

_____

_____

_____

_____

_____

_____

_____

_____

_____

_____

6. **THINKING CRITICALLY.** Use the following two-column journal to spur your thinking about the reading. In the left column record statements or paraphrased ideas from the reading that you want to explore. In the right column, write your reactions, comments, or questions. Feel free to disagree, challenge, and offer alternative viewpoints. See the inside back cover of this journal for "Ten Ways to Stimulate Your Critical Thinking and Journal Writing."

READING SELECTION	YOUR RESPONSE
(Para. __)	
(Para. __)	
(Para. __)	
(Para. __)	
(Para. __)	
(Para. __)	
(Para. __)	

7.   CHOOSING A LEARNING STRATEGY. Assume you had to take an exam based on this textbook excerpt. What learning strategies would you use?

   Learning Strategies: 1. _____

   2. _____

   3. _____

8.   PREDICTING AN ESSAY EXAM QUESTION. Assume you were going to take an essay exam based, in part, on this excerpt. What question(s) would you predict?

   Essay Exam Questions: 1. _____

   2. _____

   3. _____

9.   RATING THE READING. Alone or working with a classmate, evaluate and rate the reading selection according to each of the following criteria. Use a scale of 1 to 5, with 1 being the lowest rating and 5 being the highest rating. (1=strongly disagree, 2=disagree, 3=uncertain, 4=agree, 5=strongly agree)

	CRITERIA	YOUR RATING
a.	The reading was interesting and informative.	_____
b.	The author made it clear what was important.	_____
c.	The author provided helpful examples and explanations.	_____
d.	The reading was well organized.	_____
e.	The author defined specialized or technical vocabulary	_____

10.   FURTHER DISCUSSION, READING, AND RESEARCH. What questions would you like to ask the author? What topics or ideas do you want to know more about?

   _____

   _____

   _____

   _____

   _____

JOURNAL ENTRY FOR A TEXTBOOK–9

Textbook Reading: _____ _____ _____
                                (title)   (page) (date)

Academic Discipline: _____

BEFORE READING

1. **PREREADING.** After you have preread the selection, describe the topics and ideas you expect it to cover. Choose one of the following methods:
    - write a list of topics you expect the reading to cover
    - write a list of questions you expect the reading to answer
    - draw a diagram or map identifying key topics
    - discuss your prereading with a classmate; summarize the ideas you predict the reading will explore.

    _____

    _____

    _____

    _____

2. **CHOOSING A TEXTBOOK READING STRATEGY.** Based on what you discovered from your prereading, decide how you will read the selection. What strategies will you use? (See the inside front cover for a list of learning strategies.) Record your choice(s) below.

    Learning Strategies: 1. _____

                                          2. _____

                                          3. _____

WHILE READING

3. **MARKING UNFAMILIAR VOCABULARY.** Use context, word parts, or a dictionary to find the meanings. Jot the words' meanings as brief notes in the margin.

AFTER READING:

4. **LEARNING VOCABULARY.** Using either index cards or the Vocabulary Log beginning on p. 165, record the unfamiliar words you marked along with their meanings.

5. **EVALUATING YOUR TEXTBOOK READING STRATEGIES.** Did the learning strategies you chose in #2 work? Write a few sentences describing what did or did not work. If a strategy did not work, try to think of reasons. What, if anything, was troublesome in the reading? Explore possible solutions.

_____

_____

_____

_____

_____

_____

_____

_____

_____

_____

6.   **THINKING CRITICALLY.**   Use the following two-column journal to spur your thinking about the reading. In the left column record statements or paraphrased ideas from the reading that you want to explore. In the right column, write your reactions, comments, or questions. Feel free to disagree, challenge, and offer alternative viewpoints. See the inside back cover of this journal for "Ten Ways to Stimulate Your Critical Thinking and Journal Writing."

READING SELECTION	YOUR RESPONSE
(Para. ___)	
(Para. ___)	
(Para. ___)	
(Para. ___)	
(Para. ___)	
(Para. ___)	
(Para. ___)	

7.   **CHOOSING A LEARNING STRATEGY.** Assume you had to take an exam based on this textbook excerpt. What learning strategies would you use?

Learning Strategies: 1. _____

2. _____

3. _____

8.   **PREDICTING AN ESSAY EXAM QUESTION.** Assume you were going to take an essay exam based, in part, on this excerpt. What question(s) would you predict?

Essay Exam Questions: 1. _____

2. _____

3. _____

9.   **RATING THE READING.** Alone or working with a classmate, evaluate and rate the reading selection according to each of the following criteria. Use a scale of 1 to 5, with 1 being the lowest rating and 5 being the highest rating. (1=strongly disagree, 2=disagree, 3=uncertain, 4=agree, 5=strongly agree)

CRITERIA	YOUR RATING
a. The reading was interesting and informative.	_____
b. The author made it clear what was important.	_____
c. The author provided helpful examples and explanations.	_____
d. The reading was well organized.	_____
e. The author defined specialized or technical vocabulary	_____

10.   **FURTHER DISCUSSION, READING, AND RESEARCH.** What questions would you like to ask the author? What topics or ideas do you want to know more about?

_____

_____

_____

_____

_____

JOURNAL ENTRY FOR A TEXTBOOK–10

Textbook Reading: _____ _____ _____
                              (title)   (page)   (date)

Academic Discipline: _____

BEFORE READING

1. **PREREADING.** After you have preread the selection, describe the topics and ideas you expect it to cover. Choose one of the following methods:
   - write a list of topics you expect the reading to cover
   - write a list of questions you expect the reading to answer
   - draw a diagram or map identifying key topics
   - discuss your prereading with a classmate; summarize the ideas you predict the reading will explore.

   _____

   _____

   _____

   _____

2. **CHOOSING A TEXTBOOK READING STRATEGY.** Based on what you discovered from your prereading, decide how you will read the selection. What strategies will you use? (See the inside front cover for a list of learning strategies.) Record your choice(s) below.

   Learning Strategies: 1. _____

   2. _____

   3. _____

WHILE READING

3.   **MARKING UNFAMILIAR VOCABULARY.** Use context, word parts, or a dictionary to find the meanings. Jot the words' meanings as brief notes in the margin.

AFTER READING:

4.   **LEARNING VOCABULARY.** Using either index cards or the Vocabulary Log beginning on p. 165, record the unfamiliar words you marked along with their meanings.

5.   **EVALUATING YOUR TEXTBOOK READING STRATEGIES.** Did the learning strategies you chose in #2 work? Write a few sentences describing what did or did not work. If a strategy did not work, try to think of reasons. What, if anything, was troublesome in the reading? Explore possible solutions.

_____

_____

_____

_____

_____

_____

_____

_____

_____

_____

Textbooks

6. **THINKING CRITICALLY.** Use the following two-column journal to spur your thinking about the reading. In the left column record statements or paraphrased ideas from the reading that you want to explore. In the right column, write your reactions, comments, or questions. Feel free to disagree, challenge, and offer alternative viewpoints. See the inside back cover of this journal for "Ten Ways to Stimulate Your Critical Thinking and Journal Writing."

READING SELECTION	YOUR RESPONSE
(Para. __)	
(Para. __)	
(Para. __)	
(Para. __)	
(Para. __)	
(Para. __)	
(Para. __)	

7.   **CHOOSING A LEARNING STRATEGY.** Assume you had to take an exam based on this textbook excerpt. What learning strategies would you use?

Learning Strategies: 1. _____

                          2. _____

                          3. _____

8.   **PREDICTING AN ESSAY EXAM QUESTION.** Assume you were going to take an essay exam based, in part, on this excerpt. What question(s) would you predict?

Essay Exam Questions: 1. _____

                          2. _____

                          3. _____

9.   **RATING THE READING.** Alone or working with a classmate, evaluate and rate the reading selection according to each of the following criteria. Use a scale of 1 to 5, with 1 being the lowest rating and 5 being the highest rating. (1=strongly disagree, 2=disagree, 3=uncertain, 4=agree, 5=strongly agree)

CRITERIA	YOUR RATING
a. The reading was interesting and informative.	_____
b. The author made it clear what was important.	_____
c. The author provided helpful examples and explanations.	_____
d. The reading was well organized.	_____
e. The author defined specialized or technical vocabulary	_____

10. **FURTHER DISCUSSION, READING, AND RESEARCH.** What questions would you like to ask the author? What topics or ideas do you want to know more about?

_____

_____

_____

_____

_____

JOURNAL ENTRY FOR A TEXTBOOK–11

Textbook Reading: _____ _____ _____
(title)   (page)   (date)

Academic Discipline: _____

BEFORE READING

1. **PREREADING.** After you have preread the selection, describe the topics
    and ideas you expect it to cover. Choose one of the following methods:
    - write a list of topics you expect the reading to cover
    - write a list of questions you expect the reading to answer
    - draw a diagram or map identifying key topics
    - discuss your prereading with a classmate; summarize the ideas you
      predict the reading will explore.

    _____

    _____

    _____

    _____

2. **CHOOSING A TEXTBOOK READING STRATEGY.** Based on what you
    discovered from your prereading, decide how you will read the selection.
    What strategies will you use? (See the inside front cover for a list of
    learning strategies.) Record your choice(s) below.

    Learning Strategies: 1. _____

    2. _____

    3. _____

WHILE READING

3.   **MARKING UNFAMILIAR VOCABULARY.** Use context, word parts, or a dictionary to find the meanings. Jot the words' meanings as brief notes in the margin.

AFTER READING:

4.   **LEARNING VOCABULARY.** Using either index cards or the Vocabulary Log beginning on p. 165, record the unfamiliar words you marked along with their meanings.

5.   **EVALUATING YOUR TEXTBOOK READING STRATEGIES.** Did the learning strategies you chose in #2 work? Write a few sentences describing what did or did not work. If a strategy did not work, try to think of reasons. What, if anything, was troublesome in the reading? Explore possible solutions.

_____

_____

_____

_____

_____

_____

_____

_____

_____

_____

6.   **THINKING CRITICALLY.**   Use the following two-column journal to spur your thinking about the reading. In the left column record statements or paraphrased ideas from the reading that you want to explore. In the right column, write your reactions, comments, or questions. Feel free to disagree, challenge, and offer alternative viewpoints. See the inside back cover of this journal for "Ten Ways to Stimulate Your Critical Thinking and Journal Writing."

READING SELECTION	YOUR RESPONSE
(Para. ___)	
(Para. ___)	
(Para. ___)	
(Para. ___)	
(Para. ___)	
(Para. ___)	
(Para. ___)	

7.   **CHOOSING A LEARNING STRATEGY.** Assume you had to take an exam based on this textbook excerpt. What learning strategies would you use?

Learning Strategies: 1. _____

2. _____

3. _____

8.   **PREDICTING AN ESSAY EXAM QUESTION.** Assume you were going to take an essay exam based, in part, on this excerpt. What question(s) would you predict?

Essay Exam Questions: 1. _____

2. _____

3. _____

9.   **RATING THE READING.** Alone or working with a classmate, evaluate and rate the reading selection according to each of the following criteria. Use a scale of 1 to 5, with 1 being the lowest rating and 5 being the highest rating. (1=strongly disagree, 2=disagree, 3=uncertain, 4=agree, 5=strongly agree)

CRITERIA	YOUR RATING
a. The reading was interesting and informative.	_____
b. The author made it clear what was important.	_____
c. The author provided helpful examples and explanations.	_____
d. The reading was well organized.	_____
e. The author defined specialized or technical vocabulary	_____

10.   **FURTHER DISCUSSION, READING, AND RESEARCH.** What questions would you like to ask the author? What topics or ideas do you want to know more about?

_____

_____

_____

_____

_____

JOURNAL ENTRY FOR A TEXTBOOK–12

Textbook Reading: _____ _____ _____
                          (title)   (page) (date)

Academic Discipline: _____

BEFORE READING

1. **PREREADING.** After you have preread the selection, describe the topics
    and ideas you expect it to cover. Choose one of the following methods:
    • write a list of topics you expect the reading to cover
    • write a list of questions you expect the reading to answer
    • draw a diagram or map identifying key topics
    • discuss your prereading with a classmate; summarize the ideas you
      predict the reading will explore.

    _____

    _____

    _____

    _____

2. **CHOOSING A TEXTBOOK READING STRATEGY.** Based on what you
    discovered from your prereading, decide how you will read the selection.
    What strategies will you use? (See the inside front cover for a list of
    learning strategies.) Record your choice(s) below.

    Learning Strategies: 1. _____

                               2. _____

                               3. _____

WHILE READING

3. **MARKING UNFAMILIAR VOCABULARY.** Use context, word parts, or a dictionary to find the meanings. Jot the words' meanings as brief notes in the margin.

AFTER READING:

4. **LEARNING VOCABULARY.** Using either index cards or the Vocabulary Log beginning on p. 165, record the unfamiliar words you marked along with their meanings.

5. **EVALUATING YOUR TEXTBOOK READING STRATEGIES.** Did the learning strategies you chose in #2 work? Write a few sentences describing what did or did not work. If a strategy did not work, try to think of reasons. What, if anything, was troublesome in the reading? Explore possible solutions.

_____

_____

_____

_____

_____

_____

_____

_____

_____

_____

_____

6. **THINKING CRITICALLY.** Use the following two-column journal to spur your thinking about the reading. In the left column record statements or paraphrased ideas from the reading that you want to explore. In the right column, write your reactions, comments, or questions. Feel free to disagree, challenge, and offer alternative viewpoints. See the inside back cover of this journal for "Ten Ways to Stimulate Your Critical Thinking and Journal Writing."

READING SELECTION	YOUR RESPONSE
(Para. ___)	
(Para. ___)	
(Para. ___)	
(Para. ___)	
(Para. ___)	
(Para. ___)	
(Para. ___)	

Textbooks

7.   **CHOOSING A LEARNING STRATEGY.** Assume you had to take an exam based on this textbook excerpt. What learning strategies would you use?

   Learning Strategies: 1. _____

   2. _____

   3. _____

8.   **PREDICTING AN ESSAY EXAM QUESTION.** Assume you were going to take an essay exam based, in part, on this excerpt. What question(s) would you predict?

   Essay Exam Questions: 1. _____

   2. _____

   3. _____

9.   **RATING THE READING.** Alone or working with a classmate, evaluate and rate the reading selection according to each of the following criteria. Use a scale of 1 to 5, with 1 being the lowest rating and 5 being the highest rating. (1=strongly disagree, 2=disagree, 3=uncertain, 4=agree, 5=strongly agree)

   CRITERIA   **YOUR RATING**
   a.   The reading was interesting and informative.   _____
   b.   The author made it clear what was important.   _____
   c.   The author provided helpful examples and explanations.   _____
   d.   The reading was well organized.   _____
   e.   The author defined specialized or technical vocabulary   _____

10.   **FURTHER DISCUSSION, READING, AND RESEARCH.** What questions would you like to ask the author? What topics or ideas do you want to know more about?

   _____

   _____

   _____

   _____

   _____

JOURNAL ENTRY FOR A TEXTBOOK–13

Textbook Reading: _____ _____ _____
(title)   (page)   (date)

Academic Discipline: _____

BEFORE READING

1. **PREREADING.** After you have preread the selection, describe the topics and ideas you expect it to cover. Choose one of the following methods:
   - write a list of topics you expect the reading to cover
   - write a list of questions you expect the reading to answer
   - draw a diagram or map identifying key topics
   - discuss your prereading with a classmate; summarize the ideas you predict the reading will explore.

   _____

   _____

   _____

   _____

2. **CHOOSING A TEXTBOOK READING STRATEGY.** Based on what you discovered from your prereading, decide how you will read the selection. What strategies will you use? (See the inside front cover for a list of learning strategies.) Record your choice(s) below.

   Learning Strategies: 1. _____

   2. _____

   3. _____

WHILE READING

3.   MARKING UNFAMILIAR VOCABULARY. Use context, word parts, or a dictionary to find the meanings. Jot the words' meanings as brief notes in the margin.

AFTER READING:

4.   LEARNING VOCABULARY. Using either index cards or the Vocabulary Log beginning on p. 165, record the unfamiliar words you marked along with their meanings.

5.   EVALUATING YOUR TEXTBOOK READING STRATEGIES.   Did the learning strategies you chose in #2 work? Write a few sentences describing what did or did not work. If a strategy did not work, try to think of reasons. What, if anything, was troublesome in the reading? Explore possible solutions.

_____

_____

_____

_____

_____

_____

_____

_____

_____

_____

6.   **THINKING CRITICALLY.** Use the following two-column journal to spur your thinking about the reading. In the left column record statements or paraphrased ideas from the reading that you want to explore. In the right column, write your reactions, comments, or questions. Feel free to disagree, challenge, and offer alternative viewpoints. See the inside back cover of this journal for "Ten Ways to Stimulate Your Critical Thinking and Journal Writing."

Textbooks

READING SELECTION	YOUR RESPONSE
(Para. __)	
(Para. __)	
(Para. __)	
(Para. __)	
(Para. __)	
(Para. __)	
(Para. __)	

7.   CHOOSING A LEARNING STRATEGY. Assume you had to take an exam based on this textbook excerpt. What learning strategies would you use?

Learning Strategies: 1. _____

                       2. _____

                       3. _____

8.   PREDICTING AN ESSAY EXAM QUESTION. Assume you were going to take an essay exam based, in part, on this excerpt. What question(s) would you predict?

Essay Exam Questions: 1. _____

                       2. _____

                       3. _____

9.   RATING THE READING. Alone or working with a classmate, evaluate and rate the reading selection according to each of the following criteria. Use a scale of 1 to 5, with 1 being the lowest rating and 5 being the highest rating. (1=strongly disagree, 2=disagree, 3=uncertain, 4=agree, 5=strongly agree)

CRITERIA	YOUR RATING
a. The reading was interesting and informative.	_____
b. The author made it clear what was important.	_____
c. The author provided helpful examples and explanations.	_____
d. The reading was well organized.	_____
e. The author defined specialized or technical vocabulary	_____

10.   FURTHER DISCUSSION, READING, AND RESEARCH. What questions would you like to ask the author? What topics or ideas do you want to know more about?

_____

_____

_____

_____

_____

JOURNAL ENTRY FOR A TEXTBOOK–14

Textbook Reading: _____ _____ _____
                              (title)   (page)   (date)

Academic Discipline: _____

BEFORE READING

1. **PREREADING.** After you have preread the selection, describe the topics
    and ideas you expect it to cover. Choose one of the following methods:
    •   write a list of topics you expect the reading to cover
    •   write a list of questions you expect the reading to answer
    •   draw a diagram or map identifying key topics
    •   discuss your prereading with a classmate; summarize the ideas you
        predict the reading will explore.

    _____

    _____

    _____

    _____

2. **CHOOSING A TEXTBOOK READING STRATEGY.** Based on what you
    discovered from your prereading, decide how you will read the selection.
    What strategies will you use? (See the inside front cover for a list of
    learning strategies.) Record your choice(s) below.

    Learning Strategies: 1. _____

                               2. _____

                               3. _____

WHILE READING

3. **MARKING UNFAMILIAR VOCABULARY.** Use context, word parts, or a dictionary to find the meanings. Jot the words' meanings as brief notes in the margin.

AFTER READING:

4. **LEARNING VOCABULARY.** Using either index cards or the Vocabulary Log beginning on p. 165, record the unfamiliar words you marked along with their meanings.

5. **EVALUATING YOUR TEXTBOOK READING STRATEGIES.** Did the learning strategies you chose in #2 work? Write a few sentences describing what did or did not work. If a strategy did not work, try to think of reasons. What, if anything, was troublesome in the reading? Explore possible solutions.

_____

_____

_____

_____

_____

_____

_____

_____

_____

_____

_____

6. **THINKING CRITICALLY.** Use the following two-column journal to spur your thinking about the reading. In the left column record statements or paraphrased ideas from the reading that you want to explore. In the right column, write your reactions, comments, or questions. Feel free to disagree, challenge, and offer alternative viewpoints. See the inside back cover of this journal for "Ten Ways to Stimulate Your Critical Thinking and Journal Writing."

READING SELECTION	YOUR RESPONSE
(Para. __)	
(Para. __)	
(Para. __)	
(Para. __)	
(Para. __)	
(Para. __)	
(Para. __)	

Textbooks

7. **CHOOSING A LEARNING STRATEGY.** Assume you had to take an exam based on this textbook excerpt. What learning strategies would you use?

    Learning Strategies: 1. _____

    2. _____

    3. _____

8. **PREDICTING AN ESSAY EXAM QUESTION.** Assume you were going to take an essay exam based, in part, on this excerpt. What question(s) would you predict?

    Essay Exam Questions: 1. _____

    2. _____

    3. _____

9. **RATING THE READING.** Alone or working with a classmate, evaluate and rate the reading selection according to each of the following criteria. Use a scale of 1 to 5, with 1 being the lowest rating and 5 being the highest rating. (1=strongly disagree, 2=disagree, 3=uncertain, 4=agree, 5=strongly agree)

CRITERIA	YOUR RATING
a. The reading was interesting and informative.	_____
b. The author made it clear what was important.	_____
c. The author provided helpful examples and explanations.	_____
d. The reading was well organized.	_____
e. The author defined specialized or technical vocabulary	_____

10. **FURTHER DISCUSSION, READING, AND RESEARCH.** What questions would you like to ask the author? What topics or ideas do you want to know more about?

    _____

    _____

    _____

    _____

    _____

JOURNAL ENTRY FOR A TEXTBOOK–15

Textbook Reading: _____ _____ _____
(title)   (page)   (date)

Academic Discipline: _____

BEFORE READING

1. **PREREADING.** After you have preread the selection, describe the topics
    and ideas you expect it to cover. Choose one of the following methods:
    •   write a list of topics you expect the reading to cover
    •   write a list of questions you expect the reading to answer
    •   draw a diagram or map identifying key topics
    •   discuss your prereading with a classmate; summarize the ideas you
        predict the reading will explore.

    _____

    _____

    _____

    _____

2. **CHOOSING A TEXTBOOK READING STRATEGY.** Based on what you
    discovered from your prereading, decide how you will read the selection.
    What strategies will you use? (See the inside front cover for a list of
    learning strategies.) Record your choice(s) below.

    Learning Strategies: 1. _____

                               2. _____

                               3. _____

WHILE READING

3.   **MARKING UNFAMILIAR VOCABULARY.** Use context, word parts, or a dictionary to find the meanings. Jot the words' meanings as brief notes in the margin.

AFTER READING:

4.   **LEARNING VOCABULARY.** Using either index cards or the Vocabulary Log beginning on p. 165, record the unfamiliar words you marked along with their meanings.

5.   **EVALUATING YOUR TEXTBOOK READING STRATEGIES.** Did the learning strategies you chose in #2 work? Write a few sentences describing what did or did not work. If a strategy did not work, try to think of reasons. What, if anything, was troublesome in the reading? Explore possible solutions.

_____

_____

_____

_____

_____

_____

_____

_____

_____

_____

6.   **THINKING CRITICALLY.**   Use the following two-column journal to spur your thinking about the reading.   In the left column record statements or paraphrased ideas from the reading that you want to explore. In the right column, write your reactions, comments, or questions.   Feel free to disagree, challenge, and offer alternative viewpoints.   See the inside back cover of this journal for "Ten Ways to Stimulate Your Critical Thinking and Journal Writing."

READING SELECTION	YOUR RESPONSE
(Para. __)	
(Para. __)	
(Para. __)	
(Para. __)	
(Para. __)	
(Para. __)	
(Para. __)	

Textbooks

7. **CHOOSING A LEARNING STRATEGY.** Assume you had to take an exam based on this textbook excerpt. What learning strategies would you use?

   Learning Strategies: 1. _____

                               2. _____

                               3. _____

8. **PREDICTING AN ESSAY EXAM QUESTION.** Assume you were going to take an essay exam based, in part, on this excerpt. What question(s) would you predict?

   Essay Exam Questions: 1. _____

                             2. _____

                             3. _____

9. **RATING THE READING.** Alone or working with a classmate, evaluate and rate the reading selection according to each of the following criteria. Use a scale of 1 to 5, with 1 being the lowest rating and 5 being the highest rating. (1=strongly disagree, 2=disagree, 3=uncertain, 4=agree, 5=strongly agree)

CRITERIA	YOUR RATING
a. The reading was interesting and informative.	_____
b. The author made it clear what was important.	_____
c. The author provided helpful examples and explanations.	_____
d. The reading was well organized.	_____
e. The author defined specialized or technical vocabulary	_____

10. **FURTHER DISCUSSION, READING, AND RESEARCH.** What questions would you like to ask the author? What topics or ideas do you want to know more about?

    _____

    _____

    _____

    _____

    _____

JOURNAL ENTRIES
FOR ARTICLES
OR ESSAYS

JOURNAL ENTRY FOR AN ARTICLE OR ESSAY–1

Article or Essay: _____ _____ _____
                                     (title)   (page)   (date)
Author: _____

Source: [check one]   ( ) Magazine   ( ) Newspaper   ( ) Web site   ( ) Book

BEFORE READING

1. **PREREADING.** After you have preread the selection, describe the topics
    and ideas you expect it to cover. Choose *one* of the following methods:
    • write a list of topics you expect the reading to cover
    • write a list of questions you expect the reading to answer
    • draw a diagram or map identifying key topics
    • discuss your prereading with a classmate; summarize the ideas you
       predict the reading will explore.

    _____

    _____

    _____

    _____

2. **CHOOSING A READING STRATEGY.** Based on what you discovered
    from your prereading, decide how you will read the selection. What
    strategies will you use? (See the inside front cover for a list of reading
    strategies.) Record your choice(s) below.

    Reading Strategies: 1. _____

                              2. _____

                              3. _____

WHILE READING

3.   **MARKING UNFAMILIAR VOCABULARY.** Use context, word parts, or a dictionary to find the meanings. Jot the words' meanings as brief notes in the margin.

AFTER READING:

4.   **LEARNING VOCABULARY.** Using either index cards or the Vocabulary Log beginning on p. 165, record the unfamiliar words you marked along with their meanings.

5.   **EVALUATING YOUR READING STRATEGIES.** Did the learning strategies you chose in #2 work? Write a few sentences describing what did or did not work. If a strategy did not work, try to think of reasons. What, if anything, was troublesome in the reading? Explore possible solutions.

_____

_____

_____

_____

_____

_____

_____

_____

_____

_____

_____

_____

6.   **THINKING CRITICALLY.**   Use the following two-column journal to spur your thinking about the reading. In the left column record statements or paraphrased ideas from the reading that you want to explore. In the right column, write your reactions, comments, or questions. Feel free to disagree, challenge, and offer alternative viewpoints. See the inside back cover of this journal for "Ten Ways to Stimulate Your Critical Thinking and Journal Writing."

ARTICLE OR ESSAY	YOUR RESPONSE
(Para. ___)	
(Para. ___)	
(Para. ___)	
(Para. ___)	
(Para. ___)	
(Para. ___)	
(Para. ___)	
(Para. ___)	

Articles/Essays

7.   **EVALUATING THE ARTICLE OR ESSAY.**   Evaluate the organization, structure, and meaning of the article or essay by answering each of the following questions.

a.   What does the title reveal about the topic of the essay?

_____

_____

_____

b.   What does the introduction accomplish?

_____

_____

_____

c.   What is the author's thesis statement? (State it in your own words.)

_____

_____

_____

d.   What types of evidence or information does the author use to support the thesis?

_____

_____

_____

e.   What does the conclusion accomplish?

_____

_____

_____

8. **RATING THE ARTICLE OR ESSAY.** Alone or working with a classmate, evaluate and rate the reading selection according to each of the following criteria. Use a scale of 1 to 5, with 1 being the lowest rating and 5 being the highest rating. (1=strongly disagree, 2=disagree, 3=uncertain, 4=agree, 5=strongly agree)

<table>
<tr><td>**CRITERIA**</td><td>**YOUR RATING**</td></tr>
<tr><td>a. The author held my interest.</td><td>_____</td></tr>
<tr><td>b. The author seemed knowledgeable and qualified to write on the subject.</td><td>_____</td></tr>
<tr><td>c. The author presented information in a clear, understandable way.</td><td>_____</td></tr>
<tr><td>d. The reading was well organized.</td><td>_____</td></tr>
<tr><td>e. The reading seemed up-to-date and current.</td><td>_____</td></tr>
<tr><td>f. The reading distinguished fact from opinion.</td><td>_____</td></tr>
<tr><td>g. The reading presented an objective, unbiased viewpoint.</td><td>_____</td></tr>
</table>

9. **FURTHER DISCUSSION, READING, AND RESEARCH.** What questions would you like to ask the author? What topics/ideas do you want to know more about?

_____

_____

_____

_____

_____

_____

_____

_____

_____

_____

Articles/Essays

JOURNAL ENTRY FOR AN ARTICLE OR ESSAY–2

Article or Essay: _____ _____ _____
                        (title)   (page) (date)
Author: _____

Source: [check one]   ( ) Magazine   ( ) Newspaper   ( ) Web site   ( ) Book

BEFORE READING

1. **PREREADING.** After you have preread the selection, describe the topics and ideas you expect it to cover. Choose *one* of the following methods:
    *   write a list of topics you expect the reading to cover
    *   write a list of questions you expect the reading to answer
    *   draw a diagram or map identifying key topics
    *   discuss your prereading with a classmate; summarize the ideas you predict the reading will explore.

    _____

    _____

    _____

    _____

2. **CHOOSING A READING STRATEGY.** Based on what you discovered from your prereading, decide how you will read the selection. What strategies will you use? (See the inside front cover for a list of reading strategies.) Record your choice(s) below.

    Reading Strategies: 1. _____

                              2. _____

                              3. _____

WHILE READING

3.   **MARKING UNFAMILIAR VOCABULARY.** Use context, word parts, or a dictionary to find the meanings. Jot the words' meanings as brief notes in the margin.

AFTER READING:

4.   **LEARNING VOCABULARY.** Using either index cards or the Vocabulary Log beginning on p. 165, record the unfamiliar words you marked along with their meanings.

5.   **EVALUATING YOUR READING STRATEGIES.** Did the learning strategies you chose in #2 work? Write a few sentences describing what did or did not work. If a strategy did not work, try to think of reasons. What, if anything, was troublesome in the reading? Explore possible solutions.

_____

_____

_____

_____

_____

_____

_____

_____

_____

_____

_____

Articles/Essays

6.   **THINKING CRITICALLY.**   Use the following two-column journal to spur your thinking about the reading. In the left column record statements or paraphrased ideas from the reading that you want to explore. In the right column, write your reactions, comments, or questions. Feel free to disagree, challenge, and offer alternative viewpoints. See the inside back cover of this journal for "Ten Ways to Stimulate Your Critical Thinking and Journal Writing."

ARTICLE OR ESSAY	YOUR RESPONSE
(Para. __)	
(Para. __)	
(Para. __)	
(Para. __)	
(Para. __)	
(Para. __)	
(Para. __)	

7. **EVALUATING THE ARTICLE OR ESSAY.** Evaluate the organization, structure, and meaning of the article or essay by answering each of the following questions.

    a. What does the title reveal about the topic of the essay?

        _____

        _____

        _____

    b. What does the introduction accomplish?

        _____

        _____

        _____

    c. What is the author's thesis statement? (State it in your own words.)

        _____

        _____

        _____

    d. What types of evidence or information does the author use to support the thesis?

        _____

        _____

        _____

    e. What does the conclusion accomplish?

        _____

        _____

        _____

Articles/Essays

8. **RATING THE ARTICLE OR ESSAY.** Alone or working with a classmate, evaluate and rate the reading selection according to each of the following criteria. Use a scale of 1 to 5, with 1 being the lowest rating and 5 being the highest rating. (1=strongly disagree, 2=disagree, 3=uncertain, 4=agree, 5=strongly agree)

CRITERIA	YOUR RATING
a. The author held my interest.	_____
b. The author seemed knowledgeable and qualified to write on the subject.	_____
c. The author presented information in a clear, understandable way.	_____
d. The reading was well organized.	_____
e. The reading seemed up-to-date and current.	_____
f. The reading distinguished fact from opinion.	_____
g. The reading presented an objective, unbiased viewpoint.	_____

9. **FURTHER DISCUSSION, READING, AND RESEARCH.** What questions would you like to ask the author? What topics/ideas do you want to know more about?

_____

_____

_____

_____

_____

_____

_____

_____

_____

_____

_____

JOURNAL ENTRY FOR AN ARTICLE OR ESSAY–3

Article or Essay: _____ _____ _____
(title)   (page)   (date)

Author: _____

Source: [check one] ( ) Magazine ( ) Newspaper ( ) Web site ( ) Book

BEFORE READING

1. **PREREADING.** After you have preread the selection, describe the topics and ideas you expect it to cover. Choose *one* of the following methods:
    * write a list of topics you expect the reading to cover
    * write a list of questions you expect the reading to answer
    * draw a diagram or map identifying key topics
    * discuss your prereading with a classmate; summarize the ideas you predict the reading will explore.

    _____

    _____

    _____

    _____

2. **CHOOSING A READING STRATEGY.** Based on what you discovered from your prereading, decide how you will read the selection. What strategies will you use? (See the inside front cover for a list of reading strategies.) Record your choice(s) below.

    Reading Strategies: 1. _____

                                        2. _____

                                        3. _____

Articles/Essays

WHILE READING

3.   **MARKING UNFAMILIAR VOCABULARY.** Use context, word parts, or a dictionary to find the meanings. Jot the words' meanings as brief notes in the margin.

AFTER READING:

4.   **LEARNING VOCABULARY.** Using either index cards or the Vocabulary Log beginning on p. 165, record the unfamiliar words you marked along with their meanings.

5.   **EVALUATING YOUR READING STRATEGIES.** Did the learning strategies you chose in #2 work? Write a few sentences describing what did or did not work. If a strategy did not work, try to think of reasons. What, if anything, was troublesome in the reading? Explore possible solutions.

_____

_____

_____

_____

_____

_____

_____

_____

_____

_____

_____

_____

6. **THINKING CRITICALLY.** Use the following two-column journal to spur your thinking about the reading. In the left column record statements or paraphrased ideas from the reading that you want to explore. In the right column, write your reactions, comments, or questions. Feel free to disagree, challenge, and offer alternative viewpoints. See the inside back cover of this journal for "Ten Ways to Stimulate Your Critical Thinking and Journal Writing."

ARTICLE OR ESSAY	YOUR RESPONSE
(Para. __)	
(Para. __)	
(Para. __)	
(Para. __)	
(Para. __)	
(Para. __)	
(Para. __)	
(Para. __)	

Articles/Essays

7. **EVALUATING THE ARTICLE OR ESSAY.** Evaluate the organization, structure, and meaning of the article or essay by answering each of the following questions.

    a. What does the title reveal about the topic of the essay?

    _____

    _____

    _____

    b. What does the introduction accomplish?

    _____

    _____

    _____

    c. What is the author's thesis statement? (State it in your own words.)

    _____

    _____

    _____

    d. What types of evidence or information does the author use to support the thesis?

    _____

    _____

    _____

    e. What does the conclusion accomplish?

    _____

    _____

    _____

8. **RATING THE ARTICLE OR ESSAY.** Alone or working with a classmate, evaluate and rate the reading selection according to each of the following criteria. Use a scale of 1 to 5, with 1 being the lowest rating and 5 being the highest rating. (1=strongly disagree, 2=disagree, 3=uncertain, 4=agree, 5=strongly agree)

CRITERIA	YOUR RATING
a. The author held my interest.	_____
b. The author seemed knowledgeable and qualified to write on the subject.	_____
c. The author presented information in a clear, understandable way.	_____
d. The reading was well organized.	_____
e. The reading seemed up-to-date and current.	_____
f. The reading distinguished fact from opinion.	_____
g. The reading presented an objective, unbiased viewpoint.	_____

9. **FURTHER DISCUSSION, READING, AND RESEARCH.** What questions would you like to ask the author? What topics/ideas do you want to know more about?

_____

_____

_____

_____

_____

_____

_____

_____

_____

_____

Articles/Essays

JOURNAL ENTRY FOR AN ARTICLE OR ESSAY–4

Article or Essay: _____ _____ _____
    (title)   (page) (date)
Author: _____

Source: [check one]   ( ) Magazine   ( ) Newspaper   ( ) Web site   ( ) Book

BEFORE READING

1. **PREREADING.** After you have preread the selection, describe the topics and ideas you expect it to cover. Choose *one* of the following methods:
    - write a list of topics you expect the reading to cover
    - write a list of questions you expect the reading to answer
    - draw a diagram or map identifying key topics
    - discuss your prereading with a classmate; summarize the ideas you predict the reading will explore.

    _____

    _____

    _____

    _____

2. **CHOOSING A READING STRATEGY.** Based on what you discovered from your prereading, decide how you will read the selection. What strategies will you use? (See the inside front cover for a list of reading strategies.) Record your choice(s) below.

    Reading Strategies: 1. _____

                              2. _____

                              3. _____

WHILE READING

3. **MARKING UNFAMILIAR VOCABULARY.** Use context, word parts, or a dictionary to find the meanings. Jot the words' meanings as brief notes in the margin.

AFTER READING:

4. **LEARNING VOCABULARY.** Using either index cards or the Vocabulary Log beginning on p. 165, record the unfamiliar words you marked along with their meanings.

5. **EVALUATING YOUR READING STRATEGIES.** Did the learning strategies you chose in #2 work? Write a few sentences describing what did or did not work. If a strategy did not work, try to think of reasons. What, if anything, was troublesome in the reading? Explore possible solutions.

Articles/Essays

_____

_____

_____

_____

_____

_____

_____

_____

_____

_____

_____

6. **THINKING CRITICALLY.**   Use the following two-column journal to spur your thinking about the reading.   In the left column record statements or paraphrased ideas from the reading that you want to explore. In the right column, write your reactions, comments, or questions.   Feel free to disagree, challenge, and offer alternative viewpoints.   See the inside back cover of this journal for "Ten Ways to Stimulate Your Critical Thinking and Journal Writing."

ARTICLE OR ESSAY	YOUR RESPONSE
(Para. __)	
(Para. __)	
(Para. __)	
(Para. __)	
(Para. __)	
(Para. __)	
(Para. __)	
(Para. __)	

7. **EVALUATING THE ARTICLE OR ESSAY.** Evaluate the organization, structure, and meaning of the article or essay by answering each of the following questions.

a. What does the title reveal about the topic of the essay?

   _____

   _____

   _____

b. What does the introduction accomplish?

   _____

   _____

   _____

c. What is the author's thesis statement? (State it in your own words.)

   _____

   _____

   _____

d. What types of evidence or information does the author use to support the thesis?

   _____

   _____

   _____

e. What does the conclusion accomplish?

   _____

   _____

   _____

Articles/Essays

8.   **RATING THE ARTICLE OR ESSAY.**   Alone or working with a classmate, evaluate and rate the reading selection according to each of the following criteria.   Use a scale of 1 to 5, with 1 being the lowest rating and 5 being the highest rating. (1=strongly disagree, 2=disagree, 3=uncertain, 4=agree, 5=strongly agree)

CRITERIA	YOUR RATING
a. The author held my interest.	_____
b. The author seemed knowledgeable and qualified to write on the subject.	_____
c. The author presented information in a clear, understandable way.	_____
d. The reading was well organized.	_____
e. The reading seemed up-to-date and current.	_____
f. The reading distinguished fact from opinion.	_____
g. The reading presented an objective, unbiased viewpoint.	_____

9.   **FURTHER DISCUSSION, READING, AND RESEARCH.**   What questions would you like to ask the author?   What topics/ideas do you want to know more about?

_____

_____

_____

_____

_____

_____

_____

_____

_____

_____

_____

JOURNAL ENTRY FOR AN ARTICLE OR ESSAY–5

Article or Essay: _____ _____ _____
                              (title)   (page) (date)

Author: _____

Source: [check one]   ( ) Magazine   ( ) Newspaper   ( ) Web site   ( ) Book

BEFORE READING

1. **PREREADING.** After you have preread the selection, describe the topics and ideas you expect it to cover. Choose *one* of the following methods:
   - write a list of topics you expect the reading to cover
   - write a list of questions you expect the reading to answer
   - draw a diagram or map identifying key topics
   - discuss your prereading with a classmate; summarize the ideas you predict the reading will explore.

   _____

   _____

   _____

   _____

2. **CHOOSING A READING STRATEGY.** Based on what you discovered from your prereading, decide how you will read the selection. What strategies will you use? (See the inside front cover for a list of reading strategies.) Record your choice(s) below.

   Reading Strategies: 1. _____

                                        2. _____

                                        3. _____

Articles/Essays

WHILE READING

3. **MARKING UNFAMILIAR VOCABULARY.** Use context, word parts, or a dictionary to find the meanings. Jot the words' meanings as brief notes in the margin.

AFTER READING:

4. **LEARNING VOCABULARY.** Using either index cards or the Vocabulary Log beginning on p. 165, record the unfamiliar words you marked along with their meanings.

5. **EVALUATING YOUR READING STRATEGIES.** Did the learning strategies you chose in #2 work? Write a few sentences describing what did or did not work. If a strategy did not work, try to think of reasons. What, if anything, was troublesome in the reading? Explore possible solutions.

_____

_____

_____

_____

_____

_____

_____

_____

_____

_____

6. **THINKING CRITICALLY.** Use the following two-column journal to spur your thinking about the reading. In the left column record statements or paraphrased ideas from the reading that you want to explore. In the right column, write your reactions, comments, or questions. Feel free to disagree, challenge, and offer alternative viewpoints. See the inside back cover of this journal for "Ten Ways to Stimulate Your Critical Thinking and Journal Writing."

ARTICLE OR ESSAY	YOUR RESPONSE
(Para. __)	
(Para. __)	
(Para. __)	
(Para. __)	
(Para. __)	
(Para. __)	
(Para. __)	
(Para. __)	

Articles/Essays

7.   **EVALUATING THE ARTICLE OR ESSAY.** Evaluate the organization, structure, and meaning of the article or essay by answering each of the following questions.

a. What does the title reveal about the topic of the essay?

_____

_____

_____

b. What does the introduction accomplish?

_____

_____

_____

c. What is the author's thesis statement? (State it in your own words.)

_____

_____

_____

d. What types of evidence or information does the author use to support the thesis?

_____

_____

_____

e. What does the conclusion accomplish?

_____

_____

_____

8. **RATING THE ARTICLE OR ESSAY.** Alone or working with a classmate, evaluate and rate the reading selection according to each of the following criteria. Use a scale of 1 to 5, with 1 being the lowest rating and 5 being the highest rating. (1=strongly disagree, 2=disagree, 3=uncertain, 4=agree, 5=strongly agree)

CRITERIA	YOUR RATING
a. The author held my interest.	_____
b. The author seemed knowledgeable and qualified to write on the subject.	_____
c. The author presented information in a clear, understandable way.	_____
d. The reading was well organized.	_____
e. The reading seemed up-to-date and current.	_____
f. The reading distinguished fact from opinion.	_____
g. The reading presented an objective, unbiased viewpoint.	_____

9. **FURTHER DISCUSSION, READING, AND RESEARCH.** What questions would you like to ask the author? What topics/ideas do you want to know more about?

_____

_____

_____

_____

_____

_____

_____

_____

_____

_____

_____

Articles/Essays

JOURNAL ENTRY FOR AN ARTICLE OR ESSAY–6

Article or Essay: _____ _____ _____
    (title)   (page)   (date)
Author: _____

Source: [check one]   ( ) Magazine   ( ) Newspaper   ( ) Web site   ( ) Book

BEFORE READING

1. **PREREADING.** After you have preread the selection, describe the topics and ideas you expect it to cover. Choose *one* of the following methods:
    - write a list of topics you expect the reading to cover
    - write a list of questions you expect the reading to answer
    - draw a diagram or map identifying key topics
    - discuss your prereading with a classmate; summarize the ideas you predict the reading will explore.

    _____

    _____

    _____

    _____

2. **CHOOSING A READING STRATEGY.** Based on what you discovered from your prereading, decide how you will read the selection. What strategies will you use? (See the inside front cover for a list of reading strategies.) Record your choice(s) below.

    Reading Strategies: 1. _____

                              2. _____

                              3. _____

WHILE READING

3. **MARKING UNFAMILIAR VOCABULARY.** Use context, word parts, or a dictionary to find the meanings. Jot the words' meanings as brief notes in the margin.

AFTER READING:

4. **LEARNING VOCABULARY.** Using either index cards or the Vocabulary Log beginning on p. 165, record the unfamiliar words you marked along with their meanings.

5. **EVALUATING YOUR READING STRATEGIES.** Did the learning strategies you chose in #2 work? Write a few sentences describing what did or did not work. If a strategy did not work, try to think of reasons. What, if anything, was troublesome in the reading? Explore possible solutions.

_____

_____

_____

_____

_____

_____

_____

_____

_____

_____

_____

Articles/Essays

6.   **THINKING CRITICALLY.**   Use the following two-column journal to spur your thinking about the reading. In the left column record statements or paraphrased ideas from the reading that you want to explore. In the right column, write your reactions, comments, or questions. Feel free to disagree, challenge, and offer alternative viewpoints. See the inside back cover of this journal for "Ten Ways to Stimulate Your Critical Thinking and Journal Writing."

ARTICLE OR ESSAY	YOUR RESPONSE
(Para. ___)	
(Para. ___)	
(Para. ___)	
(Para. ___)	
(Para. ___)	
(Para. ___)	
(Para. ___)	
(Para. ___)	

7. **EVALUATING THE ARTICLE OR ESSAY.** Evaluate the organization, structure, and meaning of the article or essay by answering each of the following questions.

a. What does the title reveal about the topic of the essay?

_____

_____

_____

b. What does the introduction accomplish?

_____

_____

_____

c. What is the author's thesis statement? (State it in your own words.)

_____

_____

_____

d. What types of evidence or information does the author use to support the thesis?

_____

_____

_____

e. What does the conclusion accomplish?

_____

_____

_____

Articles/Essays

8.   **RATING THE ARTICLE OR ESSAY.** Alone or working with a classmate, evaluate and rate the reading selection according to each of the following criteria. Use a scale of 1 to 5, with 1 being the lowest rating and 5 being the highest rating. (1=strongly disagree, 2=disagree, 3=uncertain, 4=agree, 5=strongly agree)

CRITERIA	YOUR RATING
a. The author held my interest.	_____
b. The author seemed knowledgeable and qualified to write on the subject.	_____
c. The author presented information in a clear, understandable way.	_____
d. The reading was well organized.	_____
e. The reading seemed up-to-date and current.	_____
f. The reading distinguished fact from opinion.	_____
g. The reading presented an objective, unbiased viewpoint.	_____

9.   **FURTHER DISCUSSION, READING, AND RESEARCH.** What questions would you like to ask the author? What topics/ideas do you want to know more about?

_____

_____

_____

_____

_____

_____

_____

_____

_____

_____

JOURNAL ENTRY FOR AN ARTICLE OR ESSAY–7

Article or Essay: _____ _____ _____
                                  (title)   (page)   (date)

Author: _____

Source: [check one] ( ) Magazine ( ) Newspaper ( ) Web site ( ) Book

Articles/Essays

BEFORE READING

1. **PREREADING.** After you have preread the selection, describe the topics and ideas you expect it to cover. Choose *one* of the following methods:
    - write a list of topics you expect the reading to cover
    - write a list of questions you expect the reading to answer
    - draw a diagram or map identifying key topics
    - discuss your prereading with a classmate; summarize the ideas you predict the reading will explore.

    _____

    _____

    _____

    _____

2. **CHOOSING A READING STRATEGY.** Based on what you discovered from your prereading, decide how you will read the selection. What strategies will you use? (See the inside front cover for a list of reading strategies.) Record your choice(s) below.

    Reading Strategies: 1. _____

                                         2. _____

                                         3. _____

WHILE READING

3.   MARKING UNFAMILIAR VOCABULARY. Use context, word parts, or a dictionary to find the meanings. Jot the words' meanings as brief notes in the margin.

AFTER READING:

4.   LEARNING VOCABULARY. Using either index cards or the Vocabulary Log beginning on p. 165, record the unfamiliar words you marked along with their meanings.

5.   EVALUATING YOUR READING STRATEGIES. Did the learning strategies you chose in #2 work? Write a few sentences describing what did or did not work. If a strategy did not work, try to think of reasons. What, if anything, was troublesome in the reading? Explore possible solutions.

_____

_____

_____

_____

_____

_____

_____

_____

_____

_____

_____

_____

6.   **THINKING CRITICALLY.**   Use the following two-column journal to spur your thinking about the reading. In the left column record statements or paraphrased ideas from the reading that you want to explore. In the right column, write your reactions, comments, or questions. Feel free to disagree, challenge, and offer alternative viewpoints. See the inside back cover of this journal for "Ten Ways to Stimulate Your Critical Thinking and Journal Writing."

ARTICLE OR ESSAY	YOUR RESPONSE
(Para. __)	
(Para. __)	
(Para. __)	
(Para. __)	
(Para. __)	
(Para. __)	
(Para. __)	
(Para. __)	

Articles/Essays

7. **EVALUATING THE ARTICLE OR ESSAY.** Evaluate the organization, structure, and meaning of the article or essay by answering each of the following questions.

a. What does the title reveal about the topic of the essay?

_____

_____

_____

b. What does the introduction accomplish?

_____

_____

_____

c. What is the author's thesis statement? (State it in your own words.)

_____

_____

_____

d. What types of evidence or information does the author use to support the thesis?

_____

_____

_____

e. What does the conclusion accomplish?

_____

_____

_____

8. **RATING THE ARTICLE OR ESSAY.** Alone or working with a classmate, evaluate and rate the reading selection according to each of the following criteria. Use a scale of 1 to 5, with 1 being the lowest rating and 5 being the highest rating. (1=strongly disagree, 2=disagree, 3=uncertain, 4=agree, 5=strongly agree)

	CRITERIA	YOUR RATING
a.	The author held my interest.	_____
b.	The author seemed knowledgeable and qualified to write on the subject.	_____
c.	The author presented information in a clear, understandable way.	_____
d.	The reading was well organized.	_____
e.	The reading seemed up-to-date and current.	_____
f.	The reading distinguished fact from opinion.	_____
g.	The reading presented an objective, unbiased viewpoint.	_____

9. **FURTHER DISCUSSION, READING, AND RESEARCH.** What questions would you like to ask the author? What topics/ideas do you want to know more about?

Articles/Essays

_____

_____

_____

_____

_____

_____

_____

_____

_____

_____

JOURNAL ENTRY FOR AN ARTICLE OR ESSAY–8

Article or Essay: _____ _____ _____
(title)   (page)   (date)

Author: _____

Source: [check one] ( ) Magazine ( ) Newspaper ( ) Web site ( ) Book

BEFORE READING

1. **PREREADING.** After you have preread the selection, describe the topics and ideas you expect it to cover. Choose *one* of the following methods:
    - write a list of topics you expect the reading to cover
    - write a list of questions you expect the reading to answer
    - draw a diagram or map identifying key topics
    - discuss your prereading with a classmate; summarize the ideas you predict the reading will explore.

    _____

    _____

    _____

    _____

2. **CHOOSING A READING STRATEGY.** Based on what you discovered from your prereading, decide how you will read the selection. What strategies will you use? (See the inside front cover for a list of reading strategies.) Record your choice(s) below.

    Reading Strategies: 1. _____

    2. _____

    3. _____

WHILE READING

3. **MARKING UNFAMILIAR VOCABULARY.** Use context, word parts, or a dictionary to find the meanings. Jot the words' meanings as brief notes in the margin.

AFTER READING:

4. **LEARNING VOCABULARY.** Using either index cards or the Vocabulary Log beginning on p. 165, record the unfamiliar words you marked along with their meanings.

5. **EVALUATING YOUR READING STRATEGIES.** Did the learning strategies you chose in #2 work? Write a few sentences describing what did or did not work. If a strategy did not work, try to think of reasons. What, if anything, was troublesome in the reading? Explore possible solutions.

_____

_____

_____

_____

_____

_____

_____

_____

_____

_____

_____

Articles/Essays

6.   **THINKING CRITICALLY.**   Use the following two-column journal to spur your thinking about the reading. In the left column record statements or paraphrased ideas from the reading that you want to explore. In the right column, write your reactions, comments, or questions. Feel free to disagree, challenge, and offer alternative viewpoints. See the inside back cover of this journal for "Ten Ways to Stimulate Your Critical Thinking and Journal Writing."

ARTICLE OR ESSAY	YOUR RESPONSE
(Para. __)	
(Para. __)	
(Para. __)	
(Para. __)	
(Para. __)	
(Para. __)	
(Para. __)	
(Para. __)	

7. **EVALUATING THE ARTICLE OR ESSAY.**   Evaluate the organization, structure, and meaning of the article or essay by answering each of the following questions.

a. What does the title reveal about the topic of the essay?

_____

_____

_____

b. What does the introduction accomplish?

_____

_____

_____

c. What is the author's thesis statement? (State it in your own words.)

_____

_____

_____

d. What types of evidence or information does the author use to support the thesis?

_____

_____

_____

e. What does the conclusion accomplish?

_____

_____

_____

8. **RATING THE ARTICLE OR ESSAY.** Alone or working with a classmate, evaluate and rate the reading selection according to each of the following criteria. Use a scale of 1 to 5, with 1 being the lowest rating and 5 being the highest rating. (1=strongly disagree, 2=disagree, 3=uncertain, 4=agree, 5=strongly agree)

	CRITERIA	YOUR RATING
a.	The author held my interest.	_____
b.	The author seemed knowledgeable and qualified to write on the subject.	_____
c.	The author presented information in a clear, understandable way.	_____
d.	The reading was well organized.	_____
e.	The reading seemed up-to-date and current.	_____
f.	The reading distinguished fact from opinion.	_____
g.	The reading presented an objective, unbiased viewpoint.	_____

9. **FURTHER DISCUSSION, READING, AND RESEARCH.** What questions would you like to ask the author? What topics/ideas do you want to know more about?

_____

_____

_____

_____

_____

_____

_____

_____

_____

_____

_____

JOURNAL ENTRY FOR AN ARTICLE OR ESSAY–9

Article or Essay: _____ _____ _____
                                (title)   (page)   (date)
Author: _____

Source: [check one] ( ) Magazine ( ) Newspaper ( ) Web site ( ) Book

BEFORE READING

1. **PREREADING.** After you have preread the selection, describe the topics and ideas you expect it to cover. Choose *one* of the following methods:
    - write a list of topics you expect the reading to cover
    - write a list of questions you expect the reading to answer
    - draw a diagram or map identifying key topics
    - discuss your prereading with a classmate; summarize the ideas you predict the reading will explore.

    _____

    _____

    _____

    _____

2. **CHOOSING A READING STRATEGY.** Based on what you discovered from your prereading, decide how you will read the selection. What strategies will you use? (See the inside front cover for a list of reading strategies.) Record your choice(s) below.

    Reading Strategies: 1. _____

                              2. _____

                              3. _____

Articles/Essays

WHILE READING

3.   **MARKING UNFAMILIAR VOCABULARY.** Use context, word parts, or a dictionary to find the meanings. Jot the words' meanings as brief notes in the margin.

AFTER READING:

4.   **LEARNING VOCABULARY.** Using either index cards or the Vocabulary Log beginning on p. 165, record the unfamiliar words you marked along with their meanings.

5.   **EVALUATING YOUR READING STRATEGIES.** Did the learning strategies you chose in #2 work? Write a few sentences describing what did or did not work. If a strategy did not work, try to think of reasons. What, if anything, was troublesome in the reading? Explore possible solutions.

_____

_____

_____

_____

_____

_____

_____

_____

_____

_____

_____

_____

6. **THINKING CRITICALLY.**   Use the following two-column journal to spur your thinking about the reading. In the left column record statements or paraphrased ideas from the reading that you want to explore. In the right column, write your reactions, comments, or questions. Feel free to disagree, challenge, and offer alternative viewpoints. See the inside back cover of this journal for "Ten Ways to Stimulate Your Critical Thinking and Journal Writing."

ARTICLE OR ESSAY	YOUR RESPONSE
(Para. __)	
(Para. __)	
(Para. __)	
(Para. __)	
(Para. __)	
(Para. __)	
(Para. __)	
(Para. __)	

Articles/Essays

7. **EVALUATING THE ARTICLE OR ESSAY.** Evaluate the organization, structure, and meaning of the article or essay by answering each of the following questions.

    a. What does the title reveal about the topic of the essay?

       _____

       _____

       _____

    b. What does the introduction accomplish?

       _____

       _____

       _____

    c. What is the author's thesis statement? (State it in your own words.)

       _____

       _____

       _____

    d. What types of evidence or information does the author use to support the thesis?

       _____

       _____

       _____

    e. What does the conclusion accomplish?

       _____

       _____

       _____

8. **RATING THE ARTICLE OR ESSAY.** Alone or working with a classmate, evaluate and rate the reading selection according to each of the following criteria. Use a scale of 1 to 5, with 1 being the lowest rating and 5 being the highest rating. (1=strongly disagree, 2=disagree, 3=uncertain, 4=agree, 5=strongly agree)

CRITERIA	YOUR RATING
a. The author held my interest.	_____
b. The author seemed knowledgeable and qualified to write on the subject.	_____
c. The author presented information in a clear, understandable way.	_____
d. The reading was well organized.	_____
e. The reading seemed up-to-date and current.	_____
f. The reading distinguished fact from opinion.	_____
g. The reading presented an objective, unbiased viewpoint.	_____

9. **FURTHER DISCUSSION, READING, AND RESEARCH.** What questions would you like to ask the author? What topics/ideas do you want to know more about?

_____

_____

_____

_____

_____

_____

_____

_____

_____

_____

_____

Articles/Essays

JOURNAL ENTRY FOR AN ARTICLE OR ESSAY–10

Article or Essay: _____ _____ _____
                                         (title)   (page)   (date)
Author: _____

Source: [check one]   ( ) Magazine   ( ) Newspaper   ( ) Web site   ( ) Book

BEFORE READING

1. **PREREADING.** After you have preread the selection, describe the topics and ideas you expect it to cover. Choose *one* of the following methods:
    - write a list of topics you expect the reading to cover
    - write a list of questions you expect the reading to answer
    - draw a diagram or map identifying key topics
    - discuss your prereading with a classmate; summarize the ideas you predict the reading will explore.

    _____

    _____

    _____

    _____

2. **CHOOSING A READING STRATEGY.** Based on what you discovered from your prereading, decide how you will read the selection. What strategies will you use? (See the inside front cover for a list of reading strategies.) Record your choice(s) below.

    Reading Strategies: 1. _____

                                            2. _____

                                            3. _____

WHILE READING

3. **MARKING UNFAMILIAR VOCABULARY.** Use context, word parts, or a dictionary to find the meanings. Jot the words' meanings as brief notes in the margin.

AFTER READING:

4. **LEARNING VOCABULARY.** Using either index cards or the Vocabulary Log beginning on p. 165, record the unfamiliar words you marked along with their meanings.

5. **EVALUATING YOUR READING STRATEGIES.** Did the learning strategies you chose in #2 work? Write a few sentences describing what did or did not work. If a strategy did not work, try to think of reasons. What, if anything, was troublesome in the reading? Explore possible solutions.

_____

_____

_____

_____

_____

_____

_____

_____

_____

_____

_____

_____

Articles/Essays

6. **THINKING CRITICALLY.** Use the following two-column journal to spur your thinking about the reading. In the left column record statements or paraphrased ideas from the reading that you want to explore. In the right column, write your reactions, comments, or questions. Feel free to disagree, challenge, and offer alternative viewpoints. See the inside back cover of this journal for "Ten Ways to Stimulate Your Critical Thinking and Journal Writing."

ARTICLE OR ESSAY	YOUR RESPONSE
(Para. ___)	
(Para. ___)	
(Para. ___)	
(Para. ___)	
(Para. ___)	
(Para. ___)	
(Para. ___)	
(Para. ___)	

7. **EVALUATING THE ARTICLE OR ESSAY.** Evaluate the organization, structure, and meaning of the article or essay by answering each of the following questions.

a. What does the title reveal about the topic of the essay?

_____

_____

_____

b. What does the introduction accomplish?

_____

_____

_____

c. What is the author's thesis statement? (State it in your own words.)

_____

_____

_____

d. What types of evidence or information does the author use to support the thesis?

_____

_____

_____

e. What does the conclusion accomplish?

_____

_____

_____

Articles/Essays

8. **RATING THE ARTICLE OR ESSAY.** Alone or working with a classmate, evaluate and rate the reading selection according to each of the following criteria. Use a scale of 1 to 5, with 1 being the lowest rating and 5 being the highest rating. (1=strongly disagree, 2=disagree, 3=uncertain, 4=agree, 5=strongly agree)

CRITERIA	YOUR RATING
a. The author held my interest.	_____
b. The author seemed knowledgeable and qualified to write on the subject.	_____
c. The author presented information in a clear, understandable way.	_____
d. The reading was well organized.	_____
e. The reading seemed up-to-date and current.	_____
f. The reading distinguished fact from opinion.	_____
g. The reading presented an objective, unbiased viewpoint.	_____

9. **FURTHER DISCUSSION, READING, AND RESEARCH.** What questions would you like to ask the author? What topics/ideas do you want to know more about?

_____

_____

_____

_____

_____

_____

_____

_____

_____

_____

JOURNAL ENTRIES
FOR LITERATURE

JOURNAL ENTRY FOR LITERATURE–1

Literary Work: _____ _____ _____
(title and author)   (page)   (date)

Type of Literature: [check one] ( ) Poem ( ) Short Story ( ) Essay
                               ( ) Novel ( ) Play

FIRST READING

1. **IDENTIFYING THE LITERAL MEANING.** After you have read the work once, answer as many of the following questions as you can. (Leave those blank that you cannot answer and return to them after your second reading.)

   a. Where and when does the work take place?

   _____

   b. Who are the primary characters and what is their relation to one another?

   _____

   c. What action is occurring, if any?

   _____

   _____

SECOND AND THIRD READINGS Read the work as many times as you need to understand it.

2. **EVALUATING YOUR UNDERSTANDING.** Assess your current level of comprehension by answering each of the following questions. If you are unable to answer some of them, reread portions of the work and then discuss your answers with a classmate.

Literature

a. Summarize the plot or action.

_____

_____

_____

_____

b. Who are the important characters? Why is each important?

_____

_____

_____

_____

c. From whose point of view is the work presented?

_____

_____

d. Describe the tone.

_____

_____

e. What is the theme (important message) the work expresses?

_____

_____

_____

_____

_____

3.   **THINKING CRITICALLY.**   Use the following two-column journal to spur your thinking about the work. In the left column record statements or paraphrased ideas from the work that you want to explore. In the right column, write your reactions, comments, or questions. Feel free to disagree, challenge, and offer alternative viewpoints. See the inside back cover of this journal for "Ten Ways to Stimulate Your Critical Thinking and Journal Writing."

LITERARY WORK	YOUR RESPONSE
(page or line __)	
(page or line __)	
(page or line __)	
(page or line __)	
(page or line __)	
(page or line __)	
(page or line __)	
(page or line __)	

4.   **EVALUATING THE LANGUAGE OF LITERATURE.**   Review the work and identify each of the following:
     a. List several words with strong connotative meanings.

     _____

     b. List several particularly descriptive words.

     _____

     c. List several examples of figurative language.

     _____

     _____

     d. What symbols are used?

     _____

AFTER READING

5.   **RATING THE WORK.** Alone or working with a classmate, evaluate and rate the work according to each of the following criteria. Use a scale of 1 to 5, with 1 being the lowest rating and 5 being the highest rating. (1=strongly disagree, 2=disagree, 3=uncertain, 4=agree, 5=strongly agree)

CRITERIA	YOUR RATING
a. The work has lasting value or importance.	_____
b. The author presented his or her ideas in a clear, understandable way.	_____
c. The work seemed relevant to the issues and problems, of today's world.	_____
d. The work expanded my thinking or simulated my imagination	_____
e. I would like to read other works by the author.	_____

6.   **FURTHER DISCUSSION, READING, AND RESEARCH.** What questions would you like to ask the author? What topics/ideas do you want to know more about?

     _____

     _____

     _____

JOURNAL ENTRY FOR LITERATURE–2

Literary Work: _____ _____ _____
                          (title and author)   (page)   (date)

Type of Literature: [check one]   ( ) Poem   ( ) Short Story   ( ) Essay
                                  ( ) Novel   ( ) Play

FIRST READING

1. **IDENTIFYING THE LITERAL MEANING.** After you have read the work
    once, answer as many of the following questions as you can. (Leave
    those blank that you cannot answer and return to them after your sec-
    ond reading.)

    a. Where and when does the work take place?

        _____

    b. Who are the primary characters and what is their relation to one
        another?

        _____

    c. What action is occurring, if any?

        _____

        _____

SECOND AND THIRD READINGS Read the work as many times as you
need to understand it.

2. **EVALUATING YOUR UNDERSTANDING.** Assess your current level
    of comprehension by answering each of the following questions. If you
    are unable to answer some of them, reread portions of the work and then
    discuss your answers with a classmate.

Literature

a. Summarize the plot or action.

_____

_____

_____

_____

b. Who are the important characters? Why is each important?

_____

_____

_____

_____

c. From whose point of view is the work presented?

_____

_____

d. Describe the tone.

_____

_____

e. What is the theme (important message) the work expresses?

_____

_____

_____

_____

3. **THINKING CRITICALLY.**   Use the following two-column journal to spur your thinking about the work. In the left column record statements or paraphrased ideas from the work that you want to explore. In the right column, write your reactions, comments, or questions. Feel free to disagree, challenge, and offer alternative viewpoints. See the inside back cover of this journal for "Ten Ways to Stimulate Your Critical Thinking and Journal Writing."

LITERARY WORK	YOUR RESPONSE
(page or line ___)	
(page or line ___)	
(page or line ___)	
(page or line ___)	
(page or line ___)	
(page or line ___)	
(page or line ___)	
(page or line ___)	

Literature

4.   **EVALUATING THE LANGUAGE OF LITERATURE.** Review the work and identify each of the following:
     a.   List several words with strong connotative meanings.

     _____

     b.   List several particularly descriptive words.

     _____

     c.   List several examples of figurative language.

     _____

     _____

     d.   What symbols are used?

     _____

AFTER READING

5.   **RATING THE WORK.** Alone or working with a classmate, evaluate and rate the work according to each of the following criteria. Use a scale of 1 to 5, with 1 being the lowest rating and 5 being the highest rating. (1=strongly disagree, 2=disagree, 3=uncertain, 4=agree, 5=strongly agree)

CRITERIA	YOUR RATING
a. The work has lasting value or importance.	_____
b. The author presented his or her ideas in a clear, understandable way.	_____
c. The work seemed relevant to the issues and problems, of today's world.	_____
d. The work expanded my thinking or simulated my imagination	_____
e. I would like to read other works by the author.	_____

6.   **FURTHER DISCUSSION, READING, AND RESEARCH.** What questions would you like to ask the author? What topics/ideas do you want to know more about?

     _____

     _____

     _____

JOURNAL ENTRY FOR LITERATURE–3

Literary Work: _____ _____ _____
                                    (title and author)   (page)   (date)

Type of Literature: [check one] ( ) Poem ( ) Short Story ( ) Essay
                                           ( ) Novel ( ) Play

FIRST READING

1. **IDENTIFYING THE LITERAL MEANING.** After you have read the work once, answer as many of the following questions as you can. (Leave those blank that you cannot answer and return to them after your second reading.)

    a. Where and when does the work take place?

        _____

    b. Who are the primary characters and what is their relation to one another?

        _____

    c. What action is occurring, if any?

        _____

        _____

SECOND AND THIRD READINGS Read the work as many times as you need to understand it.

2. **EVALUATING YOUR UNDERSTANDING.** Assess your current level of comprehension by answering each of the following questions. If you are unable to answer some of them, reread portions of the work and then discuss your answers with a classmate.

Literature

a. Summarize the plot or action.

_____

_____

_____

_____

b. Who are the important characters? Why is each important?

_____

_____

_____

_____

c. From whose point of view is the work presented?

_____

_____

d. Describe the tone.

_____

_____

e. What is the theme (important message) the work expresses?

_____

_____

_____

_____

_____

3. **THINKING CRITICALLY.** Use the following two-column journal to spur your thinking about the work. In the left column record statements or paraphrased ideas from the work that you want to explore. In the right column, write your reactions, comments, or questions. Feel free to disagree, challenge, and offer alternative viewpoints. See the inside back cover of this journal for "Ten Ways to Stimulate Your Critical Thinking and Journal Writing."

LITERARY WORK	YOUR RESPONSE
(page or line __)	
(page or line __)	
(page or line __)	
(page or line __)	
(page or line __)	
(page or line __)	
(page or line __)	
(page or line __)	

Literature

4.   **EVALUATING THE LANGUAGE OF LITERATURE.**   Review the work and identify each of the following:

a.   List several words with strong connotative meanings.

_____

b.   List several particularly descriptive words.

_____

c.   List several examples of figurative language.

_____

_____

d.   What symbols are used?

_____

AFTER READING

5.   **RATING THE WORK.**   Alone or working with a classmate, evaluate and rate the work according to each of the following criteria. Use a scale of 1 to 5, with 1 being the lowest rating and 5 being the highest rating. (1=strongly disagree, 2=disagree, 3=uncertain, 4=agree, 5=strongly agree)

CRITERIA	YOUR RATING
a. The work has lasting value or importance.	_____
b. The author presented his or her ideas in a clear, understandable way.	_____
c. The work seemed relevant to the issues and problems, of today's world.	_____
d. The work expanded my thinking or simulated my imagination	_____
e. I would like to read other works by the author.	_____

6.   **FURTHER DISCUSSION, READING, AND RESEARCH.**   What questions would you like to ask the author? What topics/ideas do you want to know more about?

_____

_____

_____

JOURNAL ENTRY FOR LITERATURE–4

Literary Work: _____ _____ _____
(title and author)   (page)   (date)

Type of Literature: [check one]   ( ) Poem   ( ) Short Story   ( ) Essay
( ) Novel   ( ) Play

FIRST READING

1. **IDENTIFYING THE LITERAL MEANING.** After you have read the work
    once, answer as many of the following questions as you can. (Leave
    those blank that you cannot answer and return to them after your sec-
    ond reading.)

    a. Where and when does the work take place?

    _____

    b. Who are the primary characters and what is their relation to one
        another?

    _____

    c. What action is occurring, if any?

    _____

    _____

SECOND AND THIRD READINGS Read the work as many times as you
need to understand it.

2. **EVALUATING YOUR UNDERSTANDING.** Assess your current level
    of comprehension by answering each of the following questions. If you
    are unable to answer some of them, reread portions of the work and then
    discuss your answers with a classmate.

Literature

a. Summarize the plot or action.

_____

_____

_____

_____

b. Who are the important characters? Why is each important?

_____

_____

_____

_____

c. From whose point of view is the work presented?

_____

_____

d. Describe the tone.

_____

_____

e. What is the theme (important message) the work expresses?

_____

_____

_____

_____

_____

3. **THINKING CRITICALLY.**   Use the following two-column journal to spur your thinking about the work. In the left column record statements or paraphrased ideas from the work that you want to explore. In the right column, write your reactions, comments, or questions. Feel free to disagree, challenge, and offer alternative viewpoints. See the inside back cover of this journal for "Ten Ways to Stimulate Your Critical Thinking and Journal Writing."

LITERARY WORK	YOUR RESPONSE
(page or line ___)	
(page or line ___)	
(page or line ___)	
(page or line ___)	
(page or line ___)	
(page or line ___)	
(page or line ___)	
(page or line ___)	

Literature

4.   **EVALUATING THE LANGUAGE OF LITERATURE.** Review the work and identify each of the following:
   a. List several words with strong connotative meanings.

   _____

   b. List several particularly descriptive words.

   _____

   c. List several examples of figurative language.

   _____

   _____

   d. What symbols are used?

   _____

AFTER READING

5.   **RATING THE WORK.** Alone or working with a classmate, evaluate and rate the work according to each of the following criteria. Use a scale of 1 to 5, with 1 being the lowest rating and 5 being the highest rating. (1=strongly disagree, 2=disagree, 3=uncertain, 4=agree, 5=strongly agree)

CRITERIA	YOUR RATING
a. The work has lasting value or importance.	_____
b. The author presented his or her ideas in a clear, understandable way.	_____
c. The work seemed relevant to the issues and problems, of today's world.	_____
d. The work expanded my thinking or simulated my imagination	_____
e. I would like to read other works by the author.	_____

6.   **FURTHER DISCUSSION, READING, AND RESEARCH.** What questions would you like to ask the author? What topics/ideas do you want to know more about?

   _____

   _____

   _____

JOURNAL ENTRY FOR LITERATURE–5

Literary Work: _____ _____ _____
                                (title and author)   (page)   (date)

Type of Literature: [check one]   ( ) Poem   ( ) Short Story   ( ) Essay
                                   ( ) Novel   ( ) Play

FIRST READING

1. **IDENTIFYING THE LITERAL MEANING.** After you have read the work once, answer as many of the following questions as you can. (Leave those blank that you cannot answer and return to them after your second reading.)

    a. Where and when does the work take place?

        _____

    b. Who are the primary characters and what is their relation to one another?

        _____

    c. What action is occurring, if any?

        _____

        _____

SECOND AND THIRD READINGS   Read the work as many times as you need to understand it.

2. **EVALUATING YOUR UNDERSTANDING.** Assess your current level of comprehension by answering each of the following questions. If you are unable to answer some of them, reread portions of the work and then discuss your answers with a classmate.

Literature

a. Summarize the plot or action.

_____

_____

_____

_____

b. Who are the important characters? Why is each important?

_____

_____

_____

_____

c. From whose point of view is the work presented?

_____

_____

d. Describe the tone.

_____

_____

e. What is the theme (important message) the work expresses?

_____

_____

_____

_____

_____

3.   **THINKING CRITICALLY.**   Use the following two-column journal to spur your thinking about the work. In the left column record statements or paraphrased ideas from the work that you want to explore. In the right column, write your reactions, comments, or questions. Feel free to disagree, challenge, and offer alternative viewpoints. See the inside back cover of this journal for "Ten Ways to Stimulate Your Critical Thinking and Journal Writing."

LITERARY WORK	YOUR RESPONSE
(page or line __)	
(page or line __)	
(page or line __)	
(page or line __)	
(page or line __)	
(page or line __)	
(page or line __)	
(page or line __)	

4.   **EVALUATING THE LANGUAGE OF LITERATURE.** Review the work and identify each of the following:

   a. List several words with strong connotative meanings.

   _____

   b. List several particularly descriptive words.

   _____

   c. List several examples of figurative language.

   _____

   _____

   d. What symbols are used?

   _____

AFTER READING

5.   **RATING THE WORK.** Alone or working with a classmate, evaluate and rate the work according to each of the following criteria. Use a scale of 1 to 5, with 1 being the lowest rating and 5 being the highest rating. (1=strongly disagree, 2=disagree, 3=uncertain, 4=agree, 5=strongly agree)

	CRITERIA	YOUR RATING
a.	The work has lasting value or importance.	_____
b.	The author presented his or her ideas in a clear, understandable way.	_____
c.	The work seemed relevant to the issues and problems, of today's world.	_____
d.	The work expanded my thinking or simulated my imagination	_____
e.	I would like to read other works by the author.	_____

6.   **FURTHER DISCUSSION, READING, AND RESEARCH.** What questions would you like to ask the author? What topics/ideas do you want to know more about?

   _____

   _____

   _____

PAGES FOR REFLECTION

*Discovery consists of seeing what everybody has seen and thinking
what nobody has thought.*
        —Albert Szent-Gyorgyi von Nagyrapolt

_____

_____

_____

_____

_____

_____

_____

_____

_____

_____

_____

_____

_____

_____

_____

_____

_____

_____

_____

Reflection

Imagination rules the world.
        —Napoleon Bonaparte

_____

_____

_____

_____

_____

_____

_____

_____

_____

_____

_____

_____

_____

_____

_____

_____

_____

_____

_____

_____

_____

A problem is a chance for you to do your best.
—Duke Ellington

_____

_____

_____

_____

_____

_____

_____

_____

_____

_____

_____

_____

_____

_____

_____

_____

_____

_____

_____

Reflection

When you can't have what you want, it's time to start wanting what you have.
  —Kathleen Sutton

_____

_____

_____

_____

_____

_____

_____

_____

_____

_____

_____

_____

_____

_____

_____

_____

_____

_____

_____

_____

_____

_____

Everyone is talented, original, and has something to say.
—Brenda Veland

In order to succeed, we must first believe that we can.
    —Michael Korda

_____

_____

_____

_____

_____

_____

_____

_____

_____

_____

_____

_____

_____

_____

_____

_____

_____

_____

_____

Always do what you are afraid to do.
  —Ralph Waldo Emerson

_____

_____

_____

_____

_____

_____

_____

_____

_____

_____

_____

_____

_____

_____

_____

_____

_____

_____

Reflection

Life shrinks or expands in accordance to one's courage.
        —Anaïs Nin

A love affair with knowledge will never end in heartbreak.
    —Michael Garrett Marino

It is never too late to be what you might have been.
    —George Eliot

VOCABULARY LOG

VOCABULARY LOG

Use these pages to record words that you want to learn. They may be words that you found in textbook excerpts, articles and essays, or literature that you have written about in this journal. Feel free to add additional words from your other courses, drawing from both textbook and lecture material. You may also include each word's pronunciation and an example of its use in a sentence, if you wish.

WORD	MEANING

WORD	MEANING

WORD	MEANING

WORD	MEANING

WORD	MEANING

WORD	MEANING

WORD	MEANING

Vocabulary

WORD	MEANING

WORD	MEANING

WORD	MEANING

WORD	MEANING

Vocabulary

WORD	MEANING

WORD	MEANING

Vocabulary

WORD	MEANING